Give Them Wings

Give Them Wings

Carol Kuykendall

Tyndale House Publishers, Wheaton, Illinois

For my family,
who allow me to share our stories:

Our almost-grown children,
Derek, Lindsay, and Kendall;

and their father, my husband, Lynn

GIVE THEM WINGS

Copyright © 1994 by Carol Kuykendall. All rights reserved. International copyright secured.

Library of Congress Cataloging-in-Publication Data

Kuykendall, Carol, 1945-
    Give them wings : preparing for the time your teen leaves home / Carol Kuykendall.
       p. cm.
    ISBN 1-56179-672-7
    1. Parent and teenager. 2. Separation (Psychology) I. Title.
HQ799.15.K89   1994
306.874—dc20
                                 93-33192
                                     CIP

A Focus on the Family Book Published by
Tyndale House Publishers, Wheaton, Illinois 60189

Unless otherwise noted, Scripture quotations are from the Holy Bible, New International Version, copyright © 1973, 1978, 1984 by the International Bible Society.

No part of this publication may be reproduced, stored in a retrieval system, or transmitted in any form or by any means—electronic, mechanical, photocopy, recording, or otherwise—without prior permission of the copyright owner.

Editor: Larry K. Weeden
Cover design: Candi Park D'Agnese

Printed in the United States of America
99 00 01 02/10 9 8 7 6 5 4 3

～ Contents ～

～ Introduction ～

This is the story of one family's journey through a major transition—the time when teenagers are growing up and leaving home. It's a tricky transition. The rules of parenting grow fuzzy as our adolescents navigate that shaky bridge between childhood and adulthood. They are trying to become people who don't need us anymore. We are trying to become parents who can accept and encourage that independence.

Our bittersweet feelings often get mixed up along the way. Sometimes I long for those days when a chubby cherub held up her arms, begging for my hug because only I could change her mood from sad to glad. Yet I get goose bumps as I watch this same cherub confidently carry on a conversation with a college professor.

We face some tough emotional jostling in this journey. If *family* is a priority and we eagerly pour ourselves into the lives of the others, watching kids leave home is difficult. The closeness we've created becomes the stumbling block we have to crawl over in the adjustment. In the midst of these feelings, I pray that my love roots and encourages them but doesn't hold them back.

We can't rely on instincts during this home stretch of active parenting. My instinct is to hold on tighter when the issues of independence come closer together and the consequences of mistakes seem greater. But I know that's the very response that thwarts my goal. I need to become more of an observer and less of a stage director.

We can't rely on our own adolescent experiences, either. Our teenagers are growing up in a world far different from the one we rah-rahed our way through in high school. It's been said that the world has undergone more significant changes in the last 50 years than in all of history up to that point. I'm alarmed by many of those changes, and I have to parent with my eyes wide open, constantly seeking God's unchanging plumb line of truth in a changing world.

The passion behind this book comes from my heart's longing to make this transition in such a way that we emerge as a family that seeks to reunite around a Thanksgiving table or at a Fourth of July celebration—not out of obligation but from a genuine desire to be together. The pattern is biblical. God calls us to raise our children in families where they are nurtured, protected, prepared, and then released to venture forth, leaving father and mother, yet remaining in loving relationship with them. How do we get from here to there? How do we go from protecting and controlling to supporting and observing? How do we cope with the emptiness when they go? I've often asked myself those questions, and this book is written around a mother's struggle for answers. I'm not an expert; I'm a parent.

We're an average family. My husband, Lynn, and I have three children. At the time of this writing, two are in their early twenties, and the other is finishing high school. Though nearly all children eventually leave home for somewhere, ours have left for college, so that's the context of my descriptions. Along the way, we've faced average problems. We're far from being a perfect family; we make plenty of mistakes; and we are still in process, because a family's journey of growth and change never ends. Some of my stories are still warm from the firing line, and I tell them with my family's permission.

Writing this book has been a spiritual journey for me, an act of daily surrender as I prayed to be, as Mother Teresa once said, "a pencil in the hand of God." I hope these words I've put on paper will encourage you through this transitional time of letting go, launching adolescents, and living at home without them.

1

A Family in Flux

I sat down one recent afternoon with a pile of this year's photographs to look for an appropriate Christmas card picture. I've always enjoyed this annual task, reminiscing as I sort through the possibilities taken during summer vacations, on the first day of school, or even around the kitchen counter at some spontaneous family celebration.

But I started with a smaller pile this year. Our nearly grown kids all had jobs, so we couldn't squeeze in a summer vacation. Only one of our three is left at home to start school. And with two away at college most of the year, Lynn and I find fewer family photo opportunities around the kitchen counter.

Still, I reminisced as I flipped through the pictures. There were several from a family hike in July, but they're too dark, because that outing turned into a night hike when 21-year-old Derek vowed we could make it all the way to the top of Green Mountain, even though we started at 6:00 P.M.

1

"No sweat!" he insisted.

I should have known better. He's the same offspring who thinks running a quick two miles in 95-degree heat at high noon is "no sweat." His words reminded me of a motto that often helps in parenting our almost-grown children. The motto advises: "Don't sweat the small stuff. Only go to blows over the biggies."

The question of whether we can make it to the top of a mountain and back before dark certainly falls into the "small stuff" category, so I hushed up most of my doubt. But as we nervously picked our way back down that slippery, rocky trail in pitch-black darkness, I had to hold my tongue and keep reminding myself that at least we were involved in a memorable, all-family activity.

I also have pictures of all three kids taking turns carrying our new puppy down the trail on that same hike. They had insisted the four-month-old golden retriever would love the exercise. "No sweat," I think Derek repeated as he helped the 30-pound puppy into the car. Again I voiced some doubt, but I added to myself that great disclaimer that covers differences of opinions with almost-grown children: *Your problem —your consequence.*

When the poor little (?) puppy fell into an exhausted heap and refused to budge in the dark, the kids began carrying him without a single word of complaint. In this case, a picture is worth a thousand words, but those photos won't work for the Christmas card, either. No one else would appreciate a picture of kids carrying a pathetic, gangly puppy down a mountain trail in the dark except a mother who wanted to say, "I told you so."

We also have a few pictures from a backpacking trip. That's another story. When our kids were younger, they rolled their eyes in disbelief at the absurd notion of strapping sleeping bags on their backs and trekking to some remote spot in the mountains to sleep for a night. But since our two older ones have gone off to college, they've been miraculously transformed. Backpacking is in. The tougher, the better. Call it role reversal, but now I've become the reluctant one, because my maturity and experience are teaching me something new about camping: *It always sounds like more fun than it really is.*

When I think about camping, I look forward to finding an idyllic campsite where I'll fall sound asleep to the comforting babble of a nearby brook and the whisper of gentle breezes in the pine trees. When I actually get to the camping spot, I usually find some marshy, rain-soaked ground with mosquitoes that keep me awake by whining in my ears all night while I toss and turn, suddenly remembering every bear-mauls-camper story I've ever heard. My hands get grimy, which makes cleaning my contact lenses impossible, and cooking meals in the wilderness is just plain hard work. I'm getting dangerously close to growing out of camping—just when our children are growing into it.

Anyway, none of the pictures from that outing will work for the Christmas card, because we look like a zombie family that's been in the backwoods for months, with scruffy beards, wild hair, and rumpled, dirty clothes. Most important, *I* look the *worst*, and as long as I choose the Christmas card picture, I won't look the worst.

As I view the little pile of rejects, I realize we've run out of options. We can't take any more family pictures—the college kids have gone back to school. And then truth starts to sink in: Maybe we've reached the end of our Christmas-card-picture days.

We are a family in flux on a journey through transition. We're a family of mostly adults instead of one with parents and children. Our all-together family gatherings are fewer and farther between, and they're often marked by the friendly differences of opinions that boil down to this bottom line: At this stage of the game, we don't always know exactly who's in charge.

I used to dread the thought of entering the season of the emptying nest. But now that I'm here, I don't mean to sound all down about it. I'm confused sometimes, but I'm less resistant and more accepting in spite of some predictable losses.

At first, I felt angry about the unfairness of it all. As Derek left home and then Lindsay, I asked God, "Why did You give us the gift of family—a circle of close relationships—and then take it away?"

Now I know He does not take family away.

He merely changes its shape.

And in the changing, we have a choice. We can resist, clinging to the past and moaning over our losses. Or we can turn our faces toward this new season with hopeful expectations. I've flip-flopped between both responses, but I'm aiming for the latter. As I look back over our journey so far, I can see some toeholds that have helped me along the way.

Anticipation is worse than reality. Isn't this true of most of life's anxieties? The hours I spend dreading my dentist appointment are much worse than my 45 minutes in the chair. My fear of making a difficult phone call is much worse than the call itself. When our children are young and desperately in need of our constant love and protection, we dread the thought of their leaving home one day. "They won't be ready, and I won't be ready," we tell ourselves passionately and rationally.

That's exactly what my friend Sue told me when I ran into her recently.

"How are you?" I asked.

"Not good," she admitted in a shaky voice. "It's Matthew, our baby. He went off to kindergarten this week, and I feel so sad. I know this sounds silly, but I feel like I'm going to blink, and suddenly our kids will be grown and gone for good." Her eyes filled with tears, and she shook her head apologetically. "See? I'm a mess!"

I smiled sympathetically, because I remember feeling exactly the same way years ago when a predictable, bittersweet milestone of independence—a child's first step, first sleep-over, or first day of school—dramatically magnified the reality of their growing up and leaving home. I especially remember the day my own "baby" skipped happily down the driveway to be swallowed up by that huge, yellow school bus that whisked her off to kindergarten with a pack of squealing children I didn't know. That bus symbolized *leaving home,* and as I walked back up the driveway alone, my life passed before me like a video on fast forward. When the movie stopped, our three children were gone, leaving me to live in that dreaded place called the empty nest.

I've never liked the term *empty nest* because it sounds so utterly . . . empty! When I was little, I looked forward to growing up, getting married, and having children, but I never thought about living in an empty nest.

When Lynn and I got married and had three children in five years, I began to dread the empty nest for three specific reasons called Derek, Lindsay, and Kendall. They totally changed my life, my passions, and my definition of myself. They became part of my very being. As a friend said, "Becoming a parent means your heart is never your own again." Writer and mother Dale Hanson Bourke warns that "becoming a mother will leave her [a woman] with an emotional wound so raw that she will be forever vulnerable."[1]

After becoming a parent, I discovered I couldn't go away, even overnight, without feeling a bit incomplete. A siren in the distance always made me wonder where my children were. Their hurt feelings of rejection wounded me deeper than any physical pain I've ever endured. In an instant, I could measure their well-being by looking into their eyes, watching them walk across a playground, or listening to their voices. And I constantly needed to feast my eyes on them for that kind of checkup, because *my* well-being depended on *their* well-being. No wonder I couldn't imagine waking up one morning and not having them around!

Oh, sure, like any young mother, I often longed for the privacy and the luxury of sleeping until *I* wanted to get up in the morning, of finishing a phone conversation without interruption, or of getting dressed all by myself. I dreamed of temporary interludes from parenting—but never of giving up the job altogether.

I dreaded the thought of my kids leaving home. Family has

always been a high priority for us, and we functioned regularly as a unit—five people together. We filled all the chairs around our dinner table. We posed for the Christmas card picture together (whether it came out well or not). We visited grandparents together. We celebrated family birthdays and Thanksgivings together. I couldn't imagine removing one person from the tableau. It would throw the whole unit off balance.

These were my dreads of years ago, but experience has shown me that dread and worry are the paralyzing emotions one conjures up while standing in the present and fretting about the possibilities of the future.

I've learned that those dreads and fears ignore the sufficiency of God, who promises to provide for our needs *when we reach our point of need,* not years in advance when we're fretting over the possibilities. To dread the thought of a kindergartner going off to college is to totally jump over and ignore what God will do in the in-between time. In *The Hiding Place,* Corrie ten Boom described how her father helped her learn this lesson when she was afraid of dying at some unknown time in the future. He used an analogy about riding to Amsterdam on the train.

> "When do I give you your ticket?" he asked.
> "Why, just before we get on the train."
> "Exactly. And our wise Father in heaven knows when we're going to need things, too. Don't run out ahead of Him, Corrie. When the time comes that some of us will have to die, you will look into your heart and find the strength you need—just in time."[2]

When the day comes for children to leave home, we're given the strength to cope—just in time.

Transitions are tough. Still, most of us parents face a difficult but temporary period of adjustment. When we love passionately, we can hurt deeply. Good-byes are tough. Change is difficult. Losses cause pain. The exit of a child, especially a first or last child, forever alters the structure of a family and the definitions of individuals. The child's physical absence leaves a gaping hole in our lives for a time and often catches us by surprise, as if we never saw it coming. Our grief is real and a necessary part of a family's journey through transition.

Admittedly, some parents accept these leave-takings less emotionally than others, partly based on their God-given personalities. According the Myers-Briggs Personality Indicator, a popular method of measuring responses to life, I am a "feeling" person, which means I instinctively respond to life on a feeling level and experience losses deeply. I also resist change. I find security in the familiar—a reliable restaurant, the same old haircut, the comfortably familiar arrangement of our living room furniture. Transitions are tough for me; I grieve greatly, but the feelings are temporary. I've learned they do pass.

God's plan is perfect. Our Creator, who divided the year into seasons and the days into mornings and nights, also divided people into families. He created this gift of a structure to offer stability and loving security in the midst of an unstable and insecure world. He intended families to be the safe haven where children are born and raised, a place where the tender shoots are nurtured until their roots grow strong and deep.

But that nurturing process has a purpose and time frame. We raise our children to leave us. We take care of them while we're teaching them to take care of themselves. We transfer freedom and responsibility from our shoulders to theirs in a slow and orderly process as they grow up. When that task nears completion, we let go, and they go off on their own. That's part of God's plan for families in the changing seasons of life.

Sometimes we get so immersed in the child-rearing period that we fail to see beyond into God's plan of changing seasons. Imagine life as a whole pie, with each season being a different wedge. The child-rearing wedge, though intense and consuming, accounts for only one fraction of that whole pie. When we're immersed in that wedge, we have little energy or vision to imagine life beyond that moment. Now that I'm on my way out of that wedge, however, I'm putting it all in better perspective. God willing, I'm apt to spend twice as many years with my adult children in other seasons as I spent actively parenting them in the child-rearing season. That motivates me to let go of the parent-child modes and move toward a mutually satisfying adult-to-adult relationship.

Another perspective is that Lynn and I will be about 50 years old when the last child leaves home, and we hope to spend maybe 25 years alone together after all the kids are gone. That's five times as many years as we spent together before they were born. That knowledge motivates me to maintain a strong marriage relationship, even in the midst of the hectic distractions of raising and launching children.

I'm also seeing something else about these seasons as I exit this one. Though I've heard it a thousand times, these familiar words suddenly have new meaning: *Enjoy these years. They pass so quickly.* They do, and that reality motivates me to squeeze all the gusto out of the remains of this present season.

Years ago, an older parent advised me to "live life with no regrets." I think that father meant I should eat my fill of peaches in August, when they're ripe and in season, so that when they disappear from the stores in September, I won't feel quite so sad. Another parent told me to "make the most of life's irretrievable moments." Surely, she meant for me to recognize and embrace those moments in each season that won't come around again. There's a Latin term for the same advice: *carpe diem*, or "seize the day." That's a good way to live.

As I linger in the last days of the child-rearing season, I'm learning that God's timing and plan are perfect, even if I don't feel that way in the midst of tough transitions. I have to let go of the old to make way for the new.

God promises new beginnings. This toehold of truth is comforting me right now. It's autumn at our house, a paradoxical season when the leaves are turning colors and falling off the trees, yet the harvest of corn, squash, and apples is abundantly rich. Something is ending, but something new is beginning.

We've just returned from taking Derek and Lindsay back to college on the West Coast. The suitcases are put away. I've answered the mail and returned the phone calls. Kendall has started high school, and on the outside, it looks as if life has returned to normal. But after a pleasant summer of being together as a family of five again, I have to face the adjustment of living with this downsized version of three once more.

Experience helps me know I'll get through this bumpy place. Since I've been here before, I know I can do it again. I miss our two older ones terribly, especially the sight of them coming through the front door or the sound of their voices in the hallway. But the feelings of loss lessen in intensity and duration. I walk past their empty bedrooms with a little less sadness each day. And when I wake up in the darkness of early morning, feeling forlorn about the ending of this season in my life, I have a remedy.

I get out of bed and watch the sunrise.

I crawl out from under the covers, pull on my jeans and a sweatshirt, get a mug of steaming coffee, and sit on the front steps of our home. I first see a soft glow gathering on the eastern horizon, and then the fingers of dawn begin to lighten the dark places all around me, as though God is turning up His rheostat on a new day. Eventually, though I can't pinpoint the exact moment, night becomes day.

As I sit there sipping my coffee in the cool morning air, I feel included in this new beginning, as if God is gently beckoning me into a new day and a new season packed with potential and thumbprints of His presence. None is more powerful than the dawn, His visible, daily reminder that out of every ending, He always creates a new beginning.

2

Bittersweet Sixteen: Keys to Independence

"*H*i, Mom!" Kendall greeted me as she opened the car door and tossed her book bag onto the backseat. "I'll drive!"

Though we'd been through this after-school ritual every day for several weeks, her statement still sounded odd to me. As I slid over to the passenger seat, I wondered how this ninth-grade child—my baby—could be old enough to drive.

This moment of truth comes to all parents sometime near the beginning of their child's high-school years. With a little piece of paper called a learner's permit, the keys to the car get passed down to a member of the younger generation—and life changes forever in that family. Nothing turns a child into an adult more quickly than car keys.

Tucked within the experience of teaching a teenager to drive, however, is a focused look at the conflicts and challenges families face as adolescents move toward independence. When a parent slides over and surrenders the spot behind the wheel, the parent surrenders *control* to that teenager. And *acquiring control* is exactly what the teenager wants and needs.

But the transfer includes some tensions.

When I pick Kendall up after school, I'm reluctant to relinquish my position behind the wheel, because I don't like giving up control. It goes against my instincts. It also scares me. I fear she's not ready. Or maybe I'm not ready. But in spite of my emotions, we both know it's time. She is almost 16.

Kendall got her learner's permit six months before her sixteenth birthday because she enrolled in a drivers training class. For several weeks, she attended lectures and spent a few hours wheeling around town with an instructor who had brakes on his side of the car and a big sign on the top that warned: STUDENT DRIVER. After that, we—her parents—got the privilege of finishing the job of teaching her to drive in real traffic on real streets.

I felt at a distinct disadvantage. My car doesn't have the same set of double brakes or a big warning sign on top, and I'm not an unemotional, objective driving instructor. I'm Kendall's mother, filled with fears about the potential dangers of driving. But I know my fears shouldn't thwart her opportunities to learn, so I showed up at the school every afternoon to let her drive home.

As she got in the car that day, she scooted the seat all the way forward so her feet could touch the gas and brake pedals. Suddenly, she looked like a child ready to drive the bumper cars at an amusement park. And gripping the wheel, her hands looked like preschool hands, still dimpled at the knuckles and more suited for playing with clay than maneuvering a car into merging traffic.

I took a deep breath and fastened my seat belt as she turned the key in the ignition, waved to a few friends, and pulled out of the parking lot—going a little too fast, I thought. She continued to pick up speed as we started down the street.

I tried to sneak a look at the speedometer without her noticing.

"I'm not *even* going the speed limit," she quickly said.

We rode in silence for at least ten seconds—until we approached an intersection.

"Kendall, don't go too fast—and watch out!" I nearly shouted, slapping both hands on the dashboard to brace myself as the green light ahead turned yellow. Kendall slammed on the brakes and screeched to a halt in the middle of an intersection we should have gone through. She groaned, put the car in reverse, and backed up.

"Mom, when you worry like that, you make me feel afraid," she said, exasperated. "Besides, I know what I'm doing!"

"I'm just trying to help you," I defended myself, wondering again about the sanity of the person who thought parents could teach their teenagers how to drive. The idea may sound good in theory, but in practice, it contains all the emotional ingredients for disaster. You take a teenager who doesn't like to accept advice from a parent and close her up in a car next to that parent who's supposed to give advice. Then you add in the fact that most teenagers drive exactly the way they live life—fearlessly and enthusiastically—while most parents react the exact way *they* live life—with a healthy sense of fear. The whole scenario spells *conflict!*

Though I started each driving session with a vow to remain calm and patient, I usually ended up looking like the mother in the cartoon taped to our refrigerator door. A smiling teenager is climbing out from behind the wheel of the car. "Thanks for the driving lesson, Mom!" he says, casually slamming the door. Meanwhile, his mother is seated on the passenger side, a look of terror frozen on her face, her feet thrust straight through the floorboards.

Kendall and I made it home from school that day, floorboards intact, but not without conflict.

The Task of Adolescence

The learner's permit period of life serves as a microcosm of the tensions in a family with teenagers, because it's a time when the task of adolescence conflicts with the task of parenthood.

Adolescence is a confusing, in-between time when teenagers feel like trapeze artists who have released the bar of childhood but are hanging in midair, reaching for the bar of adulthood. In adolescence, they no longer have the privileges or excuses of childhood, but they don't yet have the freedom or independence of adulthood. Someone has called it the "un age"—unable to be an adult, unable to be a child, yet wanting to be both. It's also a bewildering time of physical changes; only the first year of life is comparable in terms of growth and changes.

The main task of adolescence, no matter how strong or close the family, is to separate, or pull away. Adolescents want to prove to themselves and others that they are individuals with personal identities separate from their families. They are seeking confidence in their ability to cope on their own. These attempts at separation are accomplished in many ways:

* asking "Who am I?" and "What do I want to be when I grow up?"
* spending more time with friends, apart from the family
* showing independence in manners of thinking or appearance
* resisting the control and authority of parents

The task of adolescence conflicts with the task of parenthood because the adolescent is trying to separate and become independent, while the parent is still trying to guide, control, and protect. No wonder adolescence is viewed as a time of upheaval!

These are some definitions I've heard:

"Adolescence is a time when teenagers fight for their independence—but that's the American way. This country was founded on the principle of fighting for independence!"

"An adolescent is like a rebellious two-year-old—with hormones and wheels."

"Adolescence is a time when parents get more difficult."

I have a button that says, "Be kind. I live with teenagers." When I wear it, I automatically get groans of sympathy, because people assume that adolescence always turns perfectly nice, easygoing children into rebellious, defiant teenagers.

Because the task of adolescence clashes with the task of parenthood during the learner's permit period of life, I came up with my own guidelines for avoiding as many sparks as possible during Kendall's training sessions. After all, I'd been through those sessions with her older brother and sister. Here are the Three R's of Teaching Teenagers to Drive:

1. Respect. Though you're in a teaching role, you're not talking to a preschooler; treat her the same way you'd like to be treated if another adult were teaching you to drive. Use "I" messages, because they sound less threatening ("I start slowing down about here"; "I look both ways even if I have the right of way"). Give encouragement and praise along with advice.

2. Rules. Stick to the important rules; don't nitpick about the routes she chooses or the length of time she leaves the turn signal on. But be sure she knows the nonmoving rules also, such as what to do in case of an emergency and where the registration, proof of insurance papers, and Hide-a-Key are kept in the car.

3. Relax. Avoid tense body language; nothing irritates a teenager more. Practice relaxation techniques like steady breathing if necessary. Pray for calmness and protection.

On the morning of Kendall's sixteenth birthday, I got up early to decorate the kitchen counter with balloons, party plates, and napkins, which has always been a family tradition. This year, however, instead of lingering over the chocolate-covered doughnuts, Kendall wanted to get to the driver's license bureau. She hoped to pass her test, drop me off at home, and then drive to school by herself.

"What if I don't pass?" she asked quietly as she drove into town extra cautiously, like a person studying for a final exam. "Laura ran a red light and failed hers. Another person hit the gas pedal instead of the brakes and ran into the back of a police car." Her voice got quieter as the threat of failure grew bigger. "I can't go to school today if I don't pass," she said.

"You'll do just fine," I assured her. Yet I felt a little nervous, too. We stepped up to the counter in the driver's license bureau, and Kendall handed her birth certificate and learner's permit to a brusque woman who peered sullenly over her glasses at us. She looked at the forms quickly, put them on a clipboard, and motioned for Kendall to follow her out a side door toward the car. I stood there helplessly, watching Kendall trot obediently behind her. Suddenly, my baby looked so small and vulnerable that I had to resist the strong urge to run after the woman and demand that she be nice to Kendall.

I sat down instead on a metal chair in the waiting area. I don't like it when circumstances beyond my control have this much power over my child's happiness. So I closed my eyes and filled my mind with a familiar image. I visually placed Kendall in the palm of my hand, cradled her tenderly for a moment, and then lifted her up with an open hand and outstretched fingers. With a silent prayer, I released her to God's plan and protection.

Place of Surrender

Within the image of releasing her to God, I walk on familiar ground, following in Abraham's footsteps up the side of a mountain called Moriah to a place of surrender. Though the setting and circumstances and the child in my hand keep changing, the path is well known to me. And each time I walk it, I'm thankful that Abraham walked it before me and his footprints show me the way. It's a path that parents must walk as we learn to relinquish our precious children, the treasures of our hearts. We might remember our first trip up the mountain most vividly, yet as we repeat the process, we begin to understand that relinquishment is not a single act. It's a lifelong attitude of the heart that roots out all sense of possessiveness and control in an openhanded, total surrender of our treasures to God.

The act of relinquishment is foundational to our faith.

Abraham was old when Isaac was born (see Gen. 21). *For a lifetime, Abraham and his wife, Sarah, longed for the child God had promised. From the moment Abraham first held Isaac in his arms, the baby became the idol of his heart. As the child grew, so did his father's love. Through protecting and caring for the precious child, Abraham bonded closer and closer until those bonds seemed to get all tangled up with his priorities and the relationship bordered on the perilous. Sometimes Abraham didn't even recognize how he was putting Isaac first.*

From the moment we knew I was pregnant, Lynn and I began to build our dreams around our longed-for first child, and the awe of his birth seemed a world-stopping moment. When the nurse handed him to us, we tenderly counted his ten perfect fingers and ten perfect toes, and we thanked God for allowing us to participate in one of His miracles. We gave our son our name; we heard others say he looked like us; we fed him, changed him, and took him to the doctor; and our passionate, protective love grew. We compared him to other babies, and in our hearts, he always rated smarter, cuter, and more responsive.

As he grew, he began to venture out to sing in a choir and make goals on the soccer team. "That's *my* boy," we each said proudly, pointing him out to others. The word *my* had a nice sound to it. He became the treasure of our hearts, and we began to do what people do with treasures. We locked our jewel in a safe-deposit box and surrounded our home with elaborate alarm systems out of fear that something might happen to our treasure. Because we worried about protecting our treasure, we held on tighter. Sometimes parents get priorities mixed up, and we forget what comes first.

After a while, God tested Abraham and said to him, "Take your son, your only son, Isaac, whom you love, and go to the region of Moriah. Sacrifice him there as a burnt offering on one of the mountains I will tell you about" (Gen. 22: 2). *Abraham obeyed and rose early the next morning, chopped wood for the fire, saddled his donkey, took his son and two servants, and started off. What agony he must have felt as he traveled for three full days, wrestling with the conflict between his feelings of overwhelming protective love for his son and his trust in God's bigger plan!*

"Wait here," he told the servants as he placed the wood on Isaac's shoulders at the foot of the mountain. Abraham picked up the knife and the flint, and father and son trudged up Mount Moriah together.

"Father, the fire and wood are here," Isaac said, "but where is the lamb for the burnt offering?"

Abraham answered, "God himself will provide the lamb for the burnt offering, my son." And the two of them went on together (Gen. 22: 8).

When our son, the treasure of our hearts, was nine years old, he was diagnosed as diabetic. For the first time in our lives, we came up against a life-threatening problem with no human solution. There was no cure—no prescription for medicine that would make him better. I felt heartbroken. Good mothers protect and take care of their children, and I couldn't fix this problem. To survive, he needed to take two shots of insulin each day, along with finger-prick blood tests. He also needed to follow a carefully monitored diet. As we all tried to adjust to the new routines, I came perilously close to turning my fears into overprotective control and tightening my fingers around his life.

"You should consider sending Derek to a week-long diabetic camp," the doctor said a few months after Derek's diagnosis. "The experience will give him confidence in his ability to take care of himself."

Derek didn't want to go. "Why are you making me go away?" he asked with tears in his eyes as we packed his clothes the night before. I hoped I wouldn't cry as I tried to help him understand—again.

"I'm afraid," he said. I was, too. We prayed together. The drive up the mountain to Shady Brook Camp seemed interminably long and quiet. As I glanced in the rearview mirror, I could see the sadness in Derek's face. He still didn't understand.

Abraham climbed to the top of the mountain, placed the wood in order for the fire, and got all the way to the point where the knife was raised above his child's head before the angel of the Lord spoke to him and stopped him.

As A. W. Tozer wrote: "God let the suffering old man go through with it up to the point where He knew there would be no retreat, and then forbade him to lay a hand upon the boy. To the wondering patriarch He now says in effect, 'It's all right, Abraham. I never intended that you should actually slay the lad. I only wanted to remove him from the temple of your heart that I might reign unchallenged there. I wanted to correct the perversion that existed in your love. Now you may have the boy, sound and well.' "[1]

Surely, as Abraham came down the mountain with his son, the words my *and* mine *meant something different to him.*

Outside a rustic camp cabin on a Sunday afternoon, we said good-bye to Derek. "We'll pick you up Saturday at 9:00 A.M.," we promised with a hug.

"Please don't be late," he pleaded as we walked away. The walk to the car became another path to a place of surrender for a mother who needed to relinquish her child. Again.

During that long week, we received a postcard. "I don't like it much here," Derek wrote. "I miss you." But on Saturday at precisely 9:00 A.M., we picked up a child who never let diabetes be the reason or excuse *not* to do something, like spend the night with a friend, run a six-mile race, or choose to go to college in another state. He gained some confidence, and I learned the meaning of relinquishment.

~~~

How many times I've followed in Abraham's footsteps up the side of Mount Moriah to that place of surrender: on the first day of school, first sleep-over, first disappointment with a friend, first attempt at a school election, first tryout for a sports team, first date—every time I've released a child to circumstances beyond my control and with an uncertain outcome.

Sometimes when I'm on the way, my fears grow too big, and I stop before I get to the place of surrender. *What if my child has an accident? What if things don't turn out right? What if my child's feelings get hurt?* And the powerful what-ifs make me turn back. So instead of an openhanded release, I wrap my fingers more tightly around my treasure, assuming for an absurd instant that I can protect my child from some circumstance or control some uncontrollable outcome. I cannot. I have only taken a detour on the path to the place of surrender.

The familiar route up Mount Moriah is marked with some guideposts of truth that Abraham left to encourage others on the same journey toward surrender. Here are three:

1. Believe God's promises. Abraham not only heard God's promises, but he also *acted* as if he believed them: "By faith Abraham, when God tested him, offered Isaac as a sacrifice" (Heb. 11:17). God promised Abraham that through his son Isaac, he would be the father of a great nation. Abraham didn't know how God would accomplish His promise—maybe God intended to raise Isaac from the dead—but he knew God would keep His promise. God has a divine love for our children that's even greater than our human love for them; He will never leave them; and He has a plan for their lives that's bigger and better than our expectations. Relinquishing our children means acknowledging God knows better than we do. In faith, we have to act as though we believe Him.

2. Recognize the surrender of our feelings. Surrendering our feelings is essential as we seek to relinquish our treasures to God's greater plan. Abraham must have struggled greatly with his feelings as he took Isaac on the three-day journey toward the place of surrender. Yet his feelings did not guide his actions; his obedience to God did. We relinquish the treasures of our hearts despite our feelings and despite the uncertain circumstances that are out of our control. We give up our self-will in seeking and accepting our loving Father's will. We also understand that our *feelings* are not more important than the *objects* of our feelings—our children—and our desire for their growth toward maturity, which happens only when we totally surrender them to God's plan.

3. What we surrender to God in faith, He gives back. Just as God gave Isaac back to Abraham, He returns our treasure to us. We may not receive it back in the same exact way, however, but in a better way from the Father who promises, "Whatever you bind on earth will be bound in heaven, and whatever you loose on earth will be loosed in heaven" (Matt. 18:18). As the late Jim Elliot said, "He is no fool who gives what he cannot keep to gain what he cannot lose."

"Mom, I passed!" Kendall's enthusiastic words jolted me back to reality as I sat in the waiting room at the driver's license bureau. "They need a check, and then we're out of here!" she said, swinging the keys around her finger. Already she looked older, more confident. I wrote the check, and Kendall traded her learner's permit for an official state of Colorado driver's license, complete with her picture and fingerprint. She didn't need me anymore. This new piece of paper gave her the legal right to drive a car in real traffic, on real streets—all by herself.

It represented a line of demarcation between childhood and adulthood.

"I can't believe it!" she squealed as we got back in the car. "I'm for *real*. I can go places all by myself!"

In no time we were home. She grabbed her book bag, gave me a hug good-bye, and rushed out the door. "See you this afternoon!" she yelled over her shoulder. And for the first time, she got in the car and drove out the driveway—alone.

I stood there at the window, watching that rear bumper disappear around the corner, and lifted my hands, palms up, with another prayer of relinquishment to God:

"Father, entering that highway of real life right now is a treasure of my heart. I've done some things wrong; I've forgotten to tell her some things. But now she's out of my control, and I surrender her to You, asking for Your loving protection, in trust and faith, even in the face of uncertain circumstances."

Letting Go: A Relinquishment Foundational to Our Faith

To let go doesn't mean to stop caring,
it means I can't do it for someone else.

To let go is not to cut myself off,
it's the realization that I can't control another.

To let go is not to enable,
but to allow learning from natural consequences.

To let go is to admit powerlessness,
which means the outcome is not in my hands.

To let go is not to try to change or blame another;
I can only change myself.

To let go is not to care for, but to care about.

To let go is not to fix, but to be supportive.

To let go is not to judge, but to allow another to be
a human being.

To let go is not to be in the middle arranging all
the outcomes, but to allow others to effect their
own outcomes.

To let go is not to be protective;
it is to permit another to face reality.

To let go is not to deny, but to accept.

To let go is not to nag, scold, or argue,
but to search out my own shortcomings and to
correct them.

To let go is not to adjust everything to my desires,
but to take each day as it comes.

To let go is not to criticize and regulate anyone,
but to try to become what I dream I can be.

To let go is not to regret the past,
but to grow and live for the future.

To let go is to fear less and love more.

— Anonymous

3

High School: New Roles, New Goals

*W*e met in a bright gymnasium on a late August evening several years ago, a bunch of parents and nervous sophomores attending a new-student orientation to learn about the expectations and requirements of high school. Lynn and I needed all the help we could get! It was our first introduction to the responsibilities of parenting a high-school student.

After the principal welcomed us, a senior offered the students some advice. "High school will be a *huge* step up, because you start facing choices that will shape the rest of your life," he told the wide-eyed group. "You begin thinking about the kind of person you want to become and what you'd like to do when you grow up. But high school zooms by quickly, so take advantage of the opportunities; try everything that interests you and a few things that don't. Sing in the choir. Try out for a play. Sign up for a random class. Learn to figure things out, but ask for help when you need it. Work hard, get involved, have fun, and make some new friends."

Next the academic counselors took over, handing out booklets with course descriptions and graduation requirements. "By the time you start high school, the date of your graduation is set," a counselor told us. "We want to help you prepare for that moment and for life after high school." He then explained the complicated but specific lists of demands in different subject areas that each student had to complete before graduation. "You need a plan," he advised, "so you get where you're supposed to be by the time graduation rolls around."

I felt a bit overwhelmed as we filed out of that warm gymnasium into the cool night air. Graduation and leaving home were no longer nebulous events floating around in a fuzzy, far-distant future. From the moment Derek entered high school, the end loomed in sight. We were embarking on a fast track to his final days at home. In my hand, I held a guide that clarified the *educational* requirements he had to complete before graduation. But what about the *emotional* requirements? We knew the goals of *schooling* him, but what about the goals of *parenting* him before he left home?

"You need a plan in order to get where you're supposed to be by the time graduation comes." Those words rang in my head as I thought about the limited time we had left to pull together the loose ends and pound home a few important messages before Derek graduated.

We needed to take stock of where we were at that point in our parenting, revise some of our goals, and come up with an updated plan aimed specifically at the final home stretch.

I started thinking about those updated goals that year, and then again as Lindsay and finally Kendall started high school a few years later. I recently wrote down those goals, and I offer my list here, not because they are inclusive or original, but because I hope my ideas might serve as a catalyst for other parents who, like me, suddenly realize their time is getting short.

I divided these goals into several parts. In this chapter, I'll focus on parenting goals: reminders of good parenting, or the basic principles that keep me on track and remind me of the bigger picture during the temporary ups and downs of the adolescent years. I'll also list my personal parenting goals, which take into account my personality traits, especially my weaknesses. In the next chapter, I'll focus on the needs of the adolescent.

Reminders of Good Parenting

1. Parenting matters during adolescence. As our children enter adolescence, we're easily pulled into the belief that since peers increasingly matter more, parenting matters less. We believe we're losing our influence. We're not. "There is no substitute for good parenting during adolescence," a sociologist friend assured me. "Teenagers need parenting based on *bonding* (knowing they are loved) and *monitoring* (knowing they have supervision and accountability)." As peer influence increases, care needs to remain consistent. We need to continue acting like their parents and offer structure and say no when necessary.

2. We must recognize the task of adolescence and enable that task rather than thwart it. The main task of adolescence is to separate, to give up dependence on parents and become increasingly independent. It is to establish a sense of self-identity by asking, "Who am I, separate from my parents?" We must vow to allow our teenagers the space and freedom to pull away, express their individuality, and begin to gain confidence in their new definitions, even though they may not always feel comfortable to us.

3. The purpose of parenting is to work ourselves out of a job.

The purpose of parenting is to care for kids in such a way that they learn how to care for themselves. Active parenting is a temporary job with planned obsolescence. Signs of independence—even our childrens' pulling away—remind us that we're doing our duty. We allow them to become people who don't need us anymore. We aim to work ourselves out of a job but not out of the relationship. We recognize that letting go has two purposes: It slowly gives them independence from us, and it also gives us independence from them so we may have the freedom to move on to new roles and challenges in the next season of life. We parent and then de-parent.

4. See them as gifts, not possessions. Psalm 127:3 states that children are *gifts*. We don't own them; they've been loaned to us temporarily to raise up and let go. They are not given to us to meet our needs and expectations. They're not here for us; we are here for them until they are grown and on their own. Their purpose in life is not to please us but to grow up and please God. We treat them with the same respect we want to receive. We don't confine them or define them with our expectations.

5. See them as separate. Though our children may look like us and sometimes act like us, they are not us. They don't need to think like us or always agree with us. They are not our clones or extensions. We're responsible to nurture and guide them as God commands, but we're not responsible for their responses. We're responsible for the process of parenting, but not for the results.

6. See them as unique. God has given us three children, and each is unique. Each has different likes and dislikes, strengths and weaknesses, dreams and goals—threads of uniqueness that weave the one-of-a-kind fabric of their souls. Prayerfully we seek to know, respect, and kindle the uniqueness of each of our kids, encouraging them to become the people God created them to be.

7. Love them unconditionally. Through this confusing time of questioning and searching for who they are, we demonstrate our love for them no matter what they look like or the decisions they make. Our love for them is not based on their performance, their appearance, or even our fickle feelings. Unconditional love means *consistently* caring for them in a way that looks out for their best interests. We want what is ultimately best for them, not what's best for us.

8. Empower them through the orderly transfer of control and responsibility. The goal is not to control them but to empower them. *Controlling* means having power over them and using external force or threats to make them behave a certain way. *Empowering* is the intentional process of building them up and enabling them to have power and control over themselves. Empowering frees them through an orderly transfer of freedom and responsibilities in such steps as:

- ❧ loosening, not tightening, the reins as they grow
- ❧ giving more information and fewer commands
- ❧ teaching them *how* to think, not *what* to think
- ❧ allowing them to make mistakes and face the consequences of their choices.

This orderly transfer demands a balance. If we don't give them enough freedom and responsibility, they will rebel and pull away to get it. If we give them too much freedom and responsibility, they will crumble, trying to act like little adults while living in high school.

Next I listed some personal goals after critically considering my own personality traits, especially the ways I might thwart my adolescents' growth toward independence. Many struggles in parenting, especially during adolescence, are based on quick, instinctive responses that become emotional stumbling blocks to doing what we know we should. This part of goal setting is more personal and focuses on some of the challenges faced in parenting almost-grown children.

Personal Parenting Goals

1. I will change. Instinctively, I resist change. Yet I know that one of the hallmarks of a Christian's life is change—changed behavior, changed perceptions, changed priorities—and I desire to be changeable. I'd like to be so open to change that I might be remembered for that quality. I would like my epitaph to read, SHE KEPT CHANGING, as opposed to the tombstone inscription I read about: DIED: AGE 30. BURIED: AGE 76.

When I was a teenager and got upset with my mother for some quirky habit, like trying to humor me out of a disappointment, she'd smile and say, "I'm sorry, honey, but you just can't change me." Surely she meant that as a joke, but I heard her saying, "I'm not willing to change" or "I don't want to change." In the midst of that statement, I felt as though my feelings didn't matter enough to change her. In parenting adolescents, willingness to change is critical, and teens need to know their feelings and opinions can effect change. Though I will never change the way I feel about them, I want to be willing to change the way I show my love for them and my expectations of the way they show their love for me. I want to be pliable in my parenting and keep changing—for the rest of my life.

2. I don't always need to be right. My husband sometimes tells me I have a stubborn need to be right. My side of the argument is the *right* side. I see the pride in that habit, and in parenting an adolescent, that trait can become a huge stumbling block. Teenagers should be allowed to have a different opinion; loving each other doesn't mean we must always agree.

During Derek's senior year, he and I had a disagreement about his priorities. An optional basketball practice conflicted with a concert he wanted to attend. I said he should go to basketball, evidencing his commitment to the team. He disagreed since the practice was optional.

"You're not right on this one, Mom, and that's good for me to know, because I used to think you were *always* right," he said.

His words saddened me, not because I'd lost that privileged (yet unrealistic) place in his heart but because I shouldn't have given him the idea that I'm always right in the first place. Only God is always right, and when I agree with God, I'm right. But in many issues, I merely have an opinion, and my almost-grown kids don't always have to agree with my view. Accepting that allows adolescents and parents to draw closer in mutually satisfying adult-to-adult relationships.

3. I will be patient. I'm not a naturally patient person. I have a hard time waiting for flowers to bloom, red lights to turn green, or someone to answer the phone when I'm put on hold. I'm especially impatient when it comes to knowing what kind of people our teenagers are becoming. I want assurance *now* that the results will be good and godly. One small sign of rebellion or self-centeredness, one bad grade, one questionable friend, or two mornings of sleeping late in a row and I'm convinced our teenagers are on an irreversible path of destruction or laziness.

I have to remember that a single piece of the puzzle does not a whole picture make, and those small blips in the path along the way may be God's way of shaping the bigger picture. I vow to be patient and let lots of pieces fill in the picture slowly instead of jumping to quick conclusions. As Solomon wrote, "The end of a matter is better than its beginning, and patience is better than pride" (Eccles. 7:8).

4. I won't let my ego get tangled up with their accomplishments. In a society where we're valued for what we produce, I sometimes let my ego get tangled up with my children's accomplishments. I'm not alone. When grade-school kids in our area make the honor roll, parents plaster bumper stickers on their cars, telling the world that "I have an honor student at Roosevelt Elementary School." Parents of college students proudly wear sweatshirts announcing the name of their son's or daughter's school, especially when that school is Princeton, Yale, or Harvard. When my daughter gets almost all *A*'s or my son climbs a tough mountain, I puff right up and want to tell my friends. Yet I have to ask myself whether I'm broadcasting their achievements to validate my success as a parent. That's as wrong as assuming their failures are my failures. Though their accomplishments make me feel proud and happy, I must not allow them to become my report cards. I must not take credit for their *A*'s or their *F*'s.

5. *I will recognize their separateness.* We are so intimately and emotionally connected to our children that sometimes the line separating us grows fuzzy. Though I list this as a reminder of good parenting, I also list it as a goal for myself, because I'm vulnerable to getting overly involved in their lives. I call it the maternal instinct, but instincts must be examined sometimes. Psychoanalyst Erich Fromm clarified that in marriage, "two people who were separate become one. In motherly love, two people who were one become separate." Then he added, "The mother must not only tolerate, she must wish and support the child's separation."[1]

I'm aware of my subtle temptations. When Derek played on the high-school tennis team, I relived the challenges of my own competitive tennis days and tried to give him too much advice. When my daughter began a relationship with a young man not long ago, the budding romance reminded me of my courtship with her dad, and in some silly way, I almost relived my own experience through hers.

Lynn calls me a wanna-be when I act as if I want to walk in their shoes. Teenagers use a different phrase. "Get a life!" they tell someone who is overly involved in the details of someone else's life. I rationalize by assuring myself I'm not as bad as the mother who followed her daughter's boyfriend to another girl's house, where he intended to work on a class project. The mother jumped out of her car and confronted the bewildered boy in the front yard. Another mother called her daughter's former boyfriend and tried to patch up their broken relationship. And we've all heard stories about some mothers' overinvolvement in their daughters' cheerleading or beauty pageant competitions. Fathers and mothers both can get overinvolved on the sidelines of their kids' sporting events. *Get a life!*

Whether it's choosing the depth of sacrifice for a competitive sport, working out the wrinkles in a peer relationship, or vowing to eat no sweets, I must let them live their own lives and be who they are, not who I wish them to be or who I wish I'd been. I must let them set and pursue goals appropriate to *their* talents and desires, not *my* expectations or dreams. I must let them be in charge of their relationships. I must allow them to look the way they choose to look. I can offer advice but not interfere or seek to control.

6. *I won't let my fears control their choices.* My children know worrying is an important part of my job description. In fact, I'm recognized as a champion worrier, because I get lots of practice and keep getting better at it. I worry even though I know the Bible is filled with commands not to worry. Here's a sampling of recent worry opportunities: When my children drive on busy freeways or narrow mountain roads, I worry. When Derek goes hiking and camping on Mount Rainier in the wintertime, I worry. When a job opportunity hangs in the balance, I worry.

I know I'm living outside the Lord's will when I worry; it shows a lack of trust in His sovereignty and diminishes my faith. I know worrying will not add a single hour to the span of my life or the lives of my children (see Matt. 6:27). I know God has a plan for their lives, as well as mine, that transcends today's circumstances. His plan for them is bigger and better than mine; it's a plan to give them "hope and a future" (Jer. 29:11). Usually, I try to look my worst fear squarely in the face and ask, "What's the *worst* thing that can happen in this situation?" Even when I imagine facing the worst, I know God is sufficient. So I cling to and claim His promises. A. W. Tozer, in *The Pursuit of God*, wrote, "Everything is safe which we commit to Him, and nothing is really safe which is not so committed."[2]

There's a second reason for not worrying. My worrying gives them a worry. If I fear for their safety as they begin a trek to Denver on the freeway, I insert that doubting, negative voice into their minds that says, *Watch out! Your mother doesn't think you can handle this! Maybe you can't.* People move in the direction of the dominant thought in their minds. If that dominant thought is *You probably can't handle this,* they are apt to fulfill that expectation.

Worrying is counterproductive to the goal of building their confidence as they seek independence. If my worry is contagious, it may influence their choices. I vow not to do that.

7. *I won't overrescue.* I'm a rescuer by nature. I'm a middle child, a zealous "fixer of all things" who likes to keep everybody happy. This personality trait tempts me to rush in and call a teacher about a seemingly unfair test or talk with a coach about a lack of playing time. By so doing, I'm trying to protect our kids from a struggle, and I have to keep reminding myself, "The lesson is in the struggle." The Bible has many examples of people who matured and grew as they struggled through adversity. Jacob did; Joseph did; David did.

In fact, as the Jewish people were on their way to the promised land, God miraculously delivered them from one crisis after another. Yet when they got to the edge of the promised land, they were afraid to enter. They had not built strength through conquering adversity. It took 40 years of wandering in the desert to prepare them for the challenges of entering the land.

Again, I can rationalize my temptation to overrescue with the comforting assurance that I'm not alone. I represent a generation of parents who are accused of protecting their children from adversity to such an extent that they don't want to grow up and face adult responsibilities. For example, I overheard a mother criticize a high-school teacher for the way he handled a discipline problem with her teenager. In the exchange, the teenager's misbehavior was totally ignored. When we divert attention from a child's behavior, we rescue him from having to face the consequences of his actions. We teach him to blame others, just as we do.

When I step in and rescue my teenagers from life's real struggles in order to make them happy, I'm buying cheap, short-term benefits at the expense of long-term lessons. I must sift through their complaints and problems and discern the valid issues that demand my involvement. And I pray I'll control my instinctive desire to rescue them from life's normal struggles and thus thwart their opportunity to grow strong.

"We must prepare the child for the road, not the road for the child," wrote pastor Earl Palmer.[3]

When I'm tempted to overrescue, I also remember the legend of the wings. It's said that birds didn't have wings in the beginning. When they first got them, they didn't like them. But once they accepted the new burden, they discovered the wings lifted them into the sky.

8. I won't manipulate by guilt. "When it comes to guilt trips, my mother wants me to be a frequent flier," I heard one teenager say. I cringed, vowing not to be remembered that way. I've always disliked manipulation through guilt. "Oh, I thought you forgot our phone number," says a mother who really means, "I miss you, and I like it when you call." But instead of speaking candidly, she falls back into the parent-controlling-child mode that says the child is supposed to please her.

Like Paul who sometimes did the very thing he hated (see Rom. 7:19), I occasionally catch myself manipulating my adolescents by guilt, which is a self-centered way to get the result I desire. And when I do it, I'm meeting my needs, not theirs. Kendall may come home from school in a silent mood. So instead of honestly admitting, "I feel sad when you come home and don't want to talk to me," I may start pulling my own silent treatment, punctuated by deep sighs and body language that shows my displeasure. By acting like a martyr, I hope to make her feel guilty about the pain she's causing me and thereby change her behavior.

Another example: I may ask my son to dump the kitchen garbage. He's watching television, but he nods, promising to do it. Instead, however, he keeps watching television. I ask two more times. Finally, I say loudly, "Okay, I guess I'll just have to do it," and I bang the garbage around as I carry it out. My actions are intended to make him feel guilty.

Manipulation by guilt is a dishonest, indirect way to express feelings, solve problems, or achieve a certain behavioral result. When I catch myself doing it, I vow to stop. I must forgive my children for not being perfect and for not perfectly fulfilling my expectations, which are sometimes unrealistic. And as they grow up, I hope they're motivated to please me—not by a sense of obligation or guilt but out of our mutual concern for one another's well-being. That motive has a chance to grow only if I pull back on my controlling demands and external manipulation by guilt. My goal is to communicate openly and honestly.

9. I won't nag. Nagging is telling someone something he already knows, like repeating commands: "Do your homework," "Call your boss," or "Get up earlier so you won't always be late." I don't want to be a nagging mother, but sometimes I hear those dreaded words coming out of my mouth.

The first time a request is made, it is informational. But when that request is repeated incessantly, it becomes nagging, which gives the negative message that an adolescent can't cope or think for himself or herself. Nagging also means something has gone wrong in the process of communication and chain of power. An adolescent may not respond to the first reminder because there is no consequence of great enough importance to motivate compliance. In our house, if completing homework is tied to car or telephone privileges, it gets done with few reminders. We have a consequence that matters.

Nagging also gets adolescents used to listening to voices outside their heads instead of inside. It removes the need to develop self-control or self-discipline, because they are used to hearing external voices giving them directions. Such kids are more susceptible to peer pressure and even cults. Kids who develop their own internal voices to direct their behavior, however, are more self-reliant. That's plenty of reason not to nag.

As I look back over this list of goals, I'm reminded of a bit of advice about goal setting: *If you aim for nothing, you're bound to hit it.* These goals, though not complete, give me something to *aim toward* as we near the end of our active parenting days. Yet I surrender them to God, praying that I'll follow them only as they fit into His plan and purpose, and that I'll be guided by His will, not my own. Apart from His wisdom and power, I can do nothing. Apart from Him, I cannot launch three adolescents into the real world.

4

Parenting: Nurturing Seeds

*W*hile our kids shuffled their way through high school, we tried to look nonchalant about placing mentors in their paths, good examples of the kinds of people they could grow up to be. We had their Young Life leaders over for dinner; we even invited 27-year-old Amy, an intern at our church, to live with us for a year.

I always studied these good examples and wondered what their parents did right. What were their secrets? What ingredients did they pour into these kids during their high-school years? What similar seeds should we be nurturing in our adolescents?

Those questions made me realize that parenting is a lot like gardening.

We identify a certain end result we want to achieve. Then we select, plant, and nurture the seeds we hope will help us reach that result. We visualize the finished product in order to know where to begin.

For parents, the finished product is an adolescent capable of coping in the real world, not because he or she will have all the answers or abilities—many of those are developed through the struggles of being away from home—but because with the right seeds growing deep within the soil of the soul, he or she will have the *potential* to manage. The investment of time and effort to nurture these seeds during high school benefits not only the adolescent, but also the parents. We can let go of our almost-grown children more easily when we believe they're ready.

The first part of this challenge comes in identifying the seeds. In their book *Leading a Child to Independence,* Paul and Jeannie McKean advise couples to take a weekend away from home to prayerfully evaluate their children's needs—spiritual, physical, intellectual, social, emotional, and financial—and come up with a step-by-step plan to help them reach maturity in each area.[1]

Lynn and I often talk about our teenagers and their growth, and as we considered the "finished products," we asked ourselves these questions: What do we want our teenagers to look like by the time they leave home? What qualities do they need to make tough decisions on their own? What character traits will equip them to withstand the storms of life outside our "greenhouse"?

Some answers came easily. We wanted them to have a yearning for God and the ability to recognize the difference between the world's messages and His. We wanted them to know the meaning of commitment and perseverance, and we wanted them to know when to say yes and when to say no. We hoped they would be both strong and tender.

Though such seeds are planted early in life, the following pages describe some of the ways those qualities can be nurtured during adolescence.

Seeds of Faith

Ultimately, our fervent prayer is that our adolescents *own their own faith*, that their spiritual lessons have become personal convictions that can grow in an environment away from the security and structure of a family and home church. Obviously, the first step toward that end is to plant the seeds of faith firmly when they are young.

We're told that God has no grandchildren, which is a catchy way of saying that kids don't get to heaven on the family plan, even if they've grown up in a Christian home. At some point, each person must make a personal commitment to Jesus Christ. Children take this step at different levels of maturity and understanding, but I hope that our adolescents leave home having surrendered what they know of themselves to what they know of Jesus Christ. According to a statistic frequently used by Billy Graham, 85 percent of all Christians give their lives to Christ by age 19.

Owning your own faith is a step beyond having personal faith. According to the youth pastor of our church, owning your faith means having the ability and desire to grow, seek, and depend upon God *in any circumstance,* even away from home or a close group of Christian friends. Many times, an adolescent's relationship with God is dependent on his or her predictable structures in a safe, comfortable environment. That's why a teenager may not own his or her own faith until that teenager leaves home.

Jacob had great lineage; he was the son of Isaac and Rebekah and a grandson of Abraham. But it wasn't until he left home, on his way to Haran in search of a wife, that he had a dream at Bethel and made his personal vow that "the Lord shall be my God." Joseph, who grew up as the favored child in a God-fearing home, didn't own his own faith until he was sold into slavery in Egypt and faced the struggles of surviving there.

Owning your own faith means reading the Bible, praying, and worshiping God out of *desire* rather than *duty.* It doesn't depend on a certain place or set of circumstances.

How do parents nurture seeds of faith and help their adolescents take steps toward owning their own faith as they grow up?
Our youth pastor offered three good suggestions:

1. *Widen their circles.* Help them understand what it means to
live "in the world but not be of the world" so they're not surprised
by the differences when they leave home. As we read the newspaper
or see ads on television, we identify how the world's priorities and
definitions of success conflict with God's. One puts self first; the
other puts God first. Don't confine high schoolers to Christian
friends and activities. Model this openness by having both
Christian and non-Christian friends from different socioeconomic
backgrounds.

2. *Encourage them to ask questions about their faith and values.*
Don't expect them to accept our answers without their own struggles.
They may ask, "How do I know God really exists? Do I have to believe
all the Bible? Is Jesus really the only way to salvation? Why does God
allow bad things to happen to innocent people?" They may question
our beliefs about church attendance or preferred forms of worship,
and they may point out examples of legalism and hypocrisy. If their
questions push our hot buttons or make them or us feel defensive,
it's best to point them to a respected outside source, such as a youth
pastor, for information.

We can also put tools in their hands. One is the book *Answers to
Tough Questions,* by Josh McDowell and Don Stewart. It clearly
addresses the kinds of questions listed above. Another tool is R. C.
Sproul's videotape series "Choosing My Religion," which tackles
head-on the questions of the MTV generation.[2] Based on interviews
with high-school and college students, some conducted during
spring break in Daytona Beach, the series challenges students to
wake up to the absolute truth found in the Bible. Students may find
this information more acceptable coming from a source other than
parents, and videos are their medium of choice.

When our teenagers bring up these subjects, we assure them

that it's okay to have questions without clear answers; that part of our faith is a mystery we won't understand until we get to heaven; and that even though those questions don't bother us, we can understand how they bother them. Many adolescents need to question their faith before they own it.

In their book *When Your Kids Aren't Kids Anymore,* Jerry and Mary White describe the way a young person develops personal beliefs: "First there is a *recognition* of the issue. Next there is the *rejection* or partial rejection of the parents' belief or value. Then there is a time of *re-evaluation.* Finally there is *rekindling* of belief or *alteration* of belief. This process takes time—often years."[3]

3. Allow them to make choices. As teens inch their way closer to independence in high school, they may ask questions like "Do I date only Christians?" Part of owning their own faith means seeking God's answers on their own while accepting advice from spiritual mentors. So we try to train them in this pattern (which goes back to the parenting goal of teaching them *how* to think, not *what* to think).

This is the way we handled the dating question: "The Bible is not clear on this issue, and it's an issue over which many Christians disagree. So when you face the situation, you might ask yourself, *What am I seeking in this relationship? And where is God in this relationship for me?* Here's my opinion: In high school, relationships are casual, and God may use you in many different relationships, but God commands you—and we care deeply—that you marry a Christian. We know that choice is way down the road, but we also know that what happens now may make a difference in that choice. We have confidence in your ability to make tough decisions, however, and this decision is yours."

In this conversation, a parent has offered advice, personal opinion, and permission for the adolescent to reach his or her own conclusion. With that combination, teenagers gain confidence in their ability to think for themselves and develop a faith that shapes their behavior.

What about the choice of going to church? What if an adolescent resists? Again, families handle this issue differently, but our youth pastor believes that during the last two years of high school, forcing teens to go to church turns church attendance into a control issue. It may increase the desire to rebel or make them more dependent on the circumstances and structure than on God.

Above all, the seeds of faith are most powerfully nourished not by church attendance, but by the consistent modeling they see at home. Teenagers carry those powerful images with them when they go out on their own.

Seeds of Confidence

What's the difference between an adolescent who looks at the floor when speaking and one who looks an adult straight in the eye? What's the difference between one who is able to speak up and voice an opinion and one who does not, or between one who tackles a problem with an I-think-I-can attitude and one who assumes "I can't do this"? The difference is *confidence,* and parents need to nurture the seeds of confidence in their adolescents as they grow.

Confidence is the internal assurance that one is valuable and capable of coping in life. Confident people define problems as "challenges I can solve." While teenagers are in high school, we need to nurture their self-confidence so they leave home with trust in their ability to make decisions.

Confidence in *themselves* is really a misnomer, however. If they have confidence only in themselves, they're relying on shallow, imperfect sources. They need confidence in God and assurance of who they are in His eyes, which gives them confidence in themselves. God's truth assures them they don't have to look or act perfect; Christ died to forgive them for being imperfect. This sets them free from bondage to self-consciousness and from believing in powerful negative, false messages: "You're fat. You're stupid. You're not good enough to get into that school."

Adolescence is a time of enormous self-consciousness, which is the opposite of self-confidence. Oprah Winfrey described adolescence as that "duck stage when everything feels awk . . . awk . . . awkward." According to a group of teenagers in our church, their greatest worries are about looks, grades, and friends. (Do people like me?)

These teens desperately need reminders about the differences between worldly priorities, which are fickle, and godly priorities, which will never let them down. ("Man looks at the outward appearance, but the LORD looks at the heart" [1 Sam. 16:7].) They need reminders that we are uniquely created in His image, with infinite value and purpose; our value, in His eyes, has nothing to do with good looks or grade point averages; He has a future of divine importance planned for each of us; and He lives within us through the person of His Holy Spirit and will never leave us.

I hope our adolescents do more than memorize these promises. I hope they *act as if they believe them.* I hope they gain confidence in themselves, not because they think they're capable of anything on their own, but because they know that the God who lives within them is powerfully capable. ("For the LORD will be your confidence" [Prov. 3:26].)

As parents of teenagers, we offer encouragement, not discouragement. I try to think before I speak and swallow words that might unnecessarily wound a teen who is already down on herself. I pass on compliments, even though I lack credibility.

"You look nice, Kendall," I say as she heads out the door.

"You have to say that. You're my mom," she replies matter-of-factly.

She's right, and that's what moms (and dads) are for.

Even though teens are busy and away from home more often, we let them know they are important to us by spending time with them, attending their events, listening to them, and showing that we respect their feelings and opinions.

We nurture their confidence in their ability to make decisions by giving them plenty of practice at making choices that aren't controlled or criticized. We give them more information and fewer commands at this stage, allowing them to decide for themselves whenever possible. We state our confidence in their ability to solve problems. "I'm curious to see how you'll handle this problem," I told Kendall when she found herself overcommitted one evening. "I know you'll come up with a good solution."

Mary gave a beautiful example of this kind of confidence in her Son when she told Him there was no more wine at the wedding in Cana (see John 2:1-11). She didn't tell Him what to do, how to do it, or when to do it; she merely gave Him the problem. Of course, Jesus had a few more resources going for Him than our kids do, but the example still holds: We can help clarify the problem and leave the solution up to them. Practice builds confidence.

Seeds of Character

We have the responsibility to nurture the seeds of character in our adolescents now more than ever, because many of our leaders are not setting good examples. Leaders who exemplify honesty, integrity, and commitment seem to be the exceptions rather than the norm. Even more disturbing is the now-common rationalization that what these leaders do in their private lives doesn't matter. That defies the definition of character I've always used: *Character is what you do when nobody else is looking.*

At maturity, strong character qualities come from internal motivation, not external controls. I hope we're nurturing qualities that will sprout in our teenagers when we're not around to remind them of the definitions. *Honesty* means telling the truth even when it doesn't matter, as well as when it will cost them. *Integrity* means being of sound moral character, having clear convictions, and doing things the right way simply because that's the way to do them, regardless of the circumstances or variables. *Commitment* means accepting responsibility and following through on your promise, even when you don't feel like it. ("Simply let your 'Yes' be

'Yes,' and your 'No,' 'No'" [Matt. 5:37].) We have commitments to our sports teams, our schools, our friends, our employers, our marriages, and our God.

Lynn and I celebrated our twenty-fifth wedding anniversary recently. As the date approached, we both felt pulled in so many directions that we didn't want to plan much of a celebration. Two comments made us change our minds.

The first came from Kendall: "Gol, Mom, in this day and age, 25 years is really worth celebrating!"

An older friend was even more direct: "You *must* make a celebration of this milestone—as much for your kids as for yourselves."

The message became clear: Being married for 25 years calls for a celebration. And as we proceeded with plans for a backyard reception, complete with music and a big cake, we watered a seed about the importance of commitment in the minds of our children. (P.S. We had a great party!)

Seeds of Perseverance

We're said to be raising the first generation of kids who won't live as well as their parents. This concerns me, not because I think they need to live as well or better but because I fear it indicates they may not be willing to work as hard. And I feel guilty when I read such predictions, because the seeds of perseverance might be the least-well-planted seeds in our adolescents. Our intentions are good, but protective parental instincts often prevail and become stumbling blocks to teaching adolescents the value of hard work and perseverance. We won't know how these seeds will sprout until our adolescents try to make it on their own in the real world, but if current studies and statistics are any indication, the cultural trend is against them. The value of hard work is not highly praised by their generation.

Life in the teen years offers many opportunities to strengthen the growing potential of these seeds. Let's use the example of participating

in high-school sports as a model for learning the value of perseverance and hard work. These are some of the battles we faced:

1. "It's too hard." The day is hot, the workout is long, and the
muscles ache. "I can't keep doing this," the teenager moans, lying
on the couch. "It's too hard. It makes me feel sick." A parent can
call the coach and complain about the tough workouts, encourage
the kid to quit so as to end the complaints, or listen with sympathy
and then encourage the teenager with some phrase he doesn't
want to hear: "Remember the greater goal down the road" or "No
pain, no gain." The truth is, all worthwhile goals demand sacrifice,
and that sacrifice often means enduring fatigue and tough workouts. Jacob worked 14 years in order to marry the woman he loved
(see Gen. 29). The idea is to keep an eye focused on the goal more
than on the struggle. ("Let us run with perseverance the race
marked out for us. Let us fix our eyes on Jesus, the author and per-
fecter of our faith" [Heb. 12:1-2].)

2. "I don't feel like doing this." It's Saturday morning—*early*—
and time to get up for practice. "I don't *feel* like going" is a true
statement. Will sleeping in once matter? A teenager can always
give the coach some believable excuse. Or does the athlete get up
and go, even though he or she doesn't feel like it? One thing I keep
learning is that a lot of life is doing what I don't *feel* like doing—
going to work, returning phone calls, cleaning the bathroom, or
pulling my hand away from another chocolate chip cookie. And
one of the greatest qualities we could nurture in our adolescents is
the seed of discipline that trains them in doing what they don't feel
like doing.

In *The Road Less Traveled,* M. Scott Peck wrote about spiritual
and mental growth toward maturity, and he identified delayed
gratification as one of the basic tools of discipline that trains us in
this area. "Delaying gratification is a process of scheduling the pain
and pleasure of life in such a way as to enhance the pleasure by
meeting and experiencing the pain first and getting it over with,"
he said.[4] Do the tough stuff first, he advised; tackle the task you

dread the most; work first and play later. This discipline is easily practiced in childhood (eat your dinner before your dessert) and through adolescence (do your homework before watching television). It trains us to do what we don't *feel* like doing. Richard Foster, a master theologian who studies and writes about spiritual disciplines, defines *discipline* as "being able to do what needs to be done when it needs to be done."

3. "I'm discouraged." In every journey toward a goal, moments of discouragement arise. In a marathon, a runner hits the famous "wall" when every muscle says, "I'm quitting." In basketball or soccer, there's a poor performance or lack of playing time. "I feel discouraged and want to quit," the player says. The parent might talk to the coach or allow the player to quit—or remind the young person that giving up won't help achieve his or her goals.

At a place of discouragement or failure, people have a choice: to allow that discouragement to weigh them down or turn it into motivation to make them better. "The only difference between stumbling blocks and steppingstones is the way you use them," I've often heard. And the only way to turn a stumbling block into a steppingstone is to not quit.

In her book *Pathfinders*, Gail Sheehy identifies a pathfinder as a person who has "confronted a crossroads, chosen a path, and emerged from the completed passage with renewed strength and expanded potential."[5] Jesus tells us that in this world, we will face storms and struggles. The seeds of perseverance might grow an adolescent into a pathfinder through those storms.

Seeds of Kindness and Compassion

I've known strong people filled with confidence, character, and perseverance but lacking in the quality of tender kindness and compassion. "If I have a faith that can move mountains, but have not love, I am nothing," Paul wrote in 1 Corinthians 13:2. The seeds of kindness (to gently care for others) and compassion (to value people and have sympathy for others' suffering) blossom into the Christian's model of love as defined by 1 Corinthians 13. They become the mournful, meek, and merciful peacemakers blessed by Jesus in the Sermon on the Mount.

How do we nurture the seeds of kindness and compassion in our adolescents, who are living through a self-conscious and therefore self-centered era of life? The most important way is to model that kind of tenderness, sensitivity, and genuine concern for one another within our families through these qualities:

1. Appreciation. This is a thank-you response to life, a demonstrated sense of gratitude for God's blessings and the kindnesses of other people. Can it be taught? Yes, starting when our children are young by insisting they say thank you and write thank-you notes, habits we hope have been ingrained by adolescence. We have lots of college kids passing through our home during the summer months. Some leave notes of gratitude that are beautiful in their sincere simplicity. But a few say nothing, which makes me realize we still have to remind our adolescents to express appreciation to others.

2. Loyalty. Kindness is expressed in the act of loyalty, or "being there for you," as teenagers say. This quality can be expressed both physically and emotionally. When Kendall took piano lessons, her teenage sister and brother tired of going to her recitals, and Kendall claimed she didn't care if they came. But just before her Christmas recital, she began worrying incessantly that she'd "mess up," so she practiced "Joy to the World" a zillion times. We all knew where her rough spots were.

"Kendall, I'm *sick* of that song!" Derek and Lindsay yelled from various parts of the house when she played. On the night of her recital at church, she said she felt ill. But Derek held her music, and Lindsay held her cold, clammy hand, and both flanked her as she walked into the sanctuary. When her turn finally came, they sat on the edges of their seats, automatically leaning forward when she approached one of her rough spots. She finally finished with a flourish, and they applauded loudly. That night, they were there for her.

3. Tenderness. The quality of tenderness is seen more in actions than in words. It's choosing to sit next to the person who is sitting alone; it's an adolescent stooping to play with a baby; it's quietly caring for all of God's creatures—a frightened child, a lost dog, or elderly grandparents. Tenderness is contagious, and we nurture the seed of tenderness when an adolescent lives with tenderness.

Seeds of Sexuality

The sexual revolution has changed the moral climate of our country, and our adolescents are growing up in a world of norms far different from those of our generation. Our task in nurturing the seeds of sexuality is to give our young people a biblical perspective on God's gift and its purpose, at the same time showing how that perspective often conflicts with contemporary values.

As adolescents reach puberty, they need information about what's happening to their bodies. They need clear role models and affirmation about their sexual identity, which is part of their "Who am I?" question. I talked with a man who grew up in a Christian family but struggled with homosexual tendencies in adolescence because he was an overly sensitive child who greatly needed affirmation from his father and didn't get it. He confused the expression of that unmet need. This young man, who is now involved in a ministry that reaches out to homosexuals and their families, claims that a "deficiency in the relationship with the same-sex parent is common for many homosexuals." We should not oversimplify a complicated subject, but sexuality in adolescence includes the establishment of clear masculine and feminine identities and role models.

Our adolescents need to know that God created the sexual differences in males and females for a purpose; that His purpose is good; and that sex between a husband and wife is good, though sex can be used for evil in this world. God intended the sexual union as a gift of intimacy and fruitfulness in marriage.

Because so many schools have sex education classes that talk more about condoms than commitment, our responsibility is to clarify the difference between love and sex. As Tony Campolo says, "True love results in right action." Dr. James Dobson's book *Preparing for Adolescence* is a helpful resource in this subject.

Seeds of Practical Coping Skills

In addition to all these seeds, from faith to sexuality, our adolescents need seeds of practical coping skills. These survival skills enable them to function in the real world away from Mom and Dad. To nurture these seeds, we first identify the areas of growth desired and then create a plan to help the adolescent master that skill, even if it means stepping back and allowing the child to fail. I had a difficult time with some of these seeds, because I used to think that a good mother takes care of her kids by washing their clothes and making hair or doctor's appointments for them. I now realize that a good parent knows when to pass such responsibilities on to her adolescents. The guideline is: Don't do for them (regularly) what they're capable of doing for themselves. These are some areas we focused on:

1. Laundry and clothing care. Our adolescents started doing their own laundry in junior high school when I realized that "cleaning their rooms" often meant putting all their clothes in the hamper. That doesn't happen when the "room cleaner" is also the "clothes washer." So they learned about sorting clothes, spot cleaning, selecting detergents, choosing the right water temperature, using bleaches and fabric softeners, and drying clothes so they don't shrink. Though they sometimes complained about these responsibilities, our two older ones now admit they are thankful that during that first year away from home, when they faced plenty of new challenges, they didn't have the added frustration of wondering how to sort clothes and select dryer temperatures.

Other basic clothes maintenance skills include knowing how to sew on buttons and mend seams, how to iron, and what to send to the dry cleaner.

2. Finances. Our teenagers got an allowance and their own checking account in high school so they could learn about budgeting, writing checks, and balancing a checkbook. Together we drew up a realistic budget and set the allowance amount by deciding which necessities they would purchase. By the end of high school, our two older ones were responsible for all their clothing purchases, toiletries, and school supplies. They learned to economize, look for sales, and recognize the difference between *want* and *need.*

3. Car maintenance. Though our two older kids don't have cars at school, car maintenance is a coping skill for life. It includes knowing how to change a tire, when and where to add oil and water, and when to schedule regular checkups. Cars need annual emissions stickers and an oil change every three months. Before any long trips, brakes, tires, and lights should be checked. Adolescents also need information about license plate registration, insurance rates, car registration, and what to do in case of an accident (get the names, phone numbers, and addresses of all persons in the other car and all witnesses, in addition to license plate number and state of registration of the other vehicle; whenever possible, notify state patrol or police officer).

4. Basic nutrition and meal preparation. During Derek's freshman year, one of his friends offered to fix dinner for them at an apartment. He tossed a two-pound bag of spaghetti into a small pot of boiling water, then couldn't figure out why he ended up with a brick of spaghetti instead of a pot full of strands. Teenagers should be able to plan and prepare at least a couple of meals (from shopping list to the table) and know the basics of nutrition, such as the importance of fruit and fiber and plenty of liquids in a diet. They should know how to read recipes, which comes from watching and doing. When one of ours made brownies for the first time and the directions said "mix by hand," that's exactly what the kid did—squishing a hand through the sticky batter in the bowl.

5. Organizational skills. Organizational skills make life more manageable. Some children are born with a greater sense of organization than others, but all can benefit from learning how to use such basic tools as desktop calendars, Day-Timers, Rolodexes, and address books. Unfortunately, few schools teach study skills, which are an excellent source of such organizational skills as how to keep track of homework assignments and deadlines; how to break large assignments into bite-sized pieces; and how to identify priorities and use time effectively. All three of our teenagers took a study skills course offered privately in our community. In his third year of college, Derek still uses the weekly/semester organization sheets he got in that class, because they help him keep track of all of his assignments, especially long-term projects, and plan his time.

6. Potpourri skills. There's a catchall bunch of skills we hope our kids learn merely by living in our home. They know, for instance, that most people change their sheets about once a week, though I have to admit that I've never heard of anyone dying of dirty sheets. (I almost died, however, when I asked Derek how many times he changed his sheets the first year of college. It reminded me of that old adage: Don't ask a question if you don't really want to know the answer!)

This list of seeds could go on, but when I imagine a garden full of these end results, I thank the Master Gardener for the privilege of being a seed planter and co-cultivator, acknowledging that the real end result is more up to Him than it is to me.

5

Adolescence:
The Yo-Yo Years

*Y*esterday seemed like a typical up-and-down day in the life of a
family with an adolescent in high school.

Shortly after Lynn left for a breakfast meeting, Kendall appeared
in the kitchen, looking about ten years older than the child I had
hugged good night just a few hours before. She wore my pale yellow blouse, her friend's chocolate brown suede skirt, and *nylons*—
a definite upgrade from her usual jeans and sweatshirt—because
she had a basketball game that day, and the players always dress up
on game days. It usually takes a combination of clothes from two
or three sources to pull together the "right" look.

I felt a funny pang as I watched her move through the kitchen. It's
not that I minded her wearing my blouse—she asked my permission.

But once in a while, when I look at her, I catch a glimpse of a woman, not a child, which both surprises and saddens me. Yet the pang had another part, too; she definitely looked better in that blouse than I do.

"I'm late, Mom," she said, grabbing a granola bar from the cupboard and pulling on her coat. She's rarely talkative and always in a hurry in the morning.

"But Kendall, you *need* to eat," I pleaded, thrusting a glass of juice at her as I followed her to the door. She turned, took a gulp (for my benefit, not hers), and with a quick good-bye was gone.

Her eating habits are an ongoing point of friction between us. I think of breakfast in terms of the four basic food groups and as the most important meal of the day; she thinks in terms of something easy to eat while on the run. Yet I try not to turn eating into a control issue—conflicts about food can lead to more serious problems, like anorexia or bulimia.

As I sat down at my desk to tackle some work projects, I thought about this yo-yo season of life. When our kids were young, I felt physically exhausted and kept telling myself that things would get better. But the adolescent years are exhausting for different reasons, and now I know that things don't get *better;* they only get *different.*

The day passed quickly, and at about 3:45, the front door opened, and a much more enthusiastic Kendall burst through it with her friend Tanna. She had an hour between school and the basketball game.

"Hi, Mom, we're starved," Kendall said, opening the refrigerator door, "but there's *nothing* to eat."

I've learned that teenagers make that statement automatically, no matter what they see in the refrigerator. I think they expect to open that door and hear a voice say, "Welcome to Taco Bell. May I take your order?"

"How about some macaroni and cheese?" I suggested.

"Great! Would you make it, Mom?" she asked eagerly.

"Sure," I answered. I don't do her laundry or clean her room—

those are her responsibilities—but I do macaroni and cheese after school, because kitchen time has the potential to become one of those rare opportunities for quality in the midst of the quantity.

"Come on, Tanna, I need to change my clothes," Kendall said, dashing my hopes. They disappeared down the hall to her room until they smelled the macaroni and cheese. While they ate, the phone rang three times. All the calls were for Kendall. I could tell from her voice that she felt excited about the game.

"We're late, Mom," she said, dashing back toward the door. "Thanks for dinner. See you at the game." And they were gone.

I've heard those alarming statistics about how many minutes parents and kids engage in eye-to-eye conversations in a day. There aren't many, and I used to cringe with guilt, wondering how adults could be so insensitive. Now I know the other side of that story, at least during the teen years. Parents can stand around like hopeful puppy dogs, waiting eagerly for their adolescents to toss them a single, teensy morsel of real conversation. And it may not happen in a whole day.

Then there's the reference to *dinner*. When I was a young mother, I vowed we'd never become one of those disconnected families that grabbed microwaved meals at the kitchen counter at odd times. No matter how busy, *dinner* meant we'd all sit down together at a table with place mats and napkins and eagerly relate the news of our days.

So much for my naive vows. Living with busy teenagers who are involved in church and school activities makes dinner together a rare celebration. Maybe that's one more way God slowly prepares us for their leaving.

As I quickly changed my clothes for the game, I paused to study myself in the mirror, and I remembered Kendall's words from a few days earlier.

"Here, Mom, let me be your fashion consultant," she offered in that half-teasing-but-I'm-really-serious voice. She then rolled up the sleeves of my jacket and bloused out my shirt before standing back to study me again. "Better," she decided, which implied "still not great."

It seemed an odd moment, reminding me of those times I used to look at her in that same critical way when she came skipping into the kitchen before preschool or Sunday school, wearing some mismatched combination of oversized clothes from her sister's closet. I could tell she thought she looked just swell, and I wondered whether my risk of embarrassment was big enough to force me to make a suggestion.

As parents, we know the importance of building our adolescents' fragile sense of self-esteem. I'm all for that, but sometimes, in self-pity, I worry that my own self-esteem is suffering under the scrutiny of my teenage daughter. I used to be *her* fashion consultant, but suddenly, she's surpassed me in knowing what is savvy, and sometimes I feel like her personal rehabilitation project.

Yet, lest I risk embarrassing Kendall at the game, I rolled my sleeves and bloused my turtleneck. "Better," I tried to convince myself.

I met Lynn at the game, and as it began, I settled down to face one of my toughest challenges: calmly watching my child play in a competitive sport. I'm a veteran who has put in plenty of time on soccer field sidelines and Little League bleachers, but the experience still baffles me. I like to think I'm normally a decent person, but I can be transformed into somebody different at those games. My palms get sweaty, my shoulders feel tense, and for some unknown reason, I can feel a passionate dislike for the loud parents of the opposing team who raise their fists and yell bad things about our team. I don't yell back, but it pushes every wrong button in me.

It turned out to be a difficult game for Kendall. She had sprained her ankle the week before, and she turned it again in the first quarter, so she sat on the bench in pain for most of the game. As I watched, I could feel her discouragement penetrating into me, which made me both mad and sad about these circumstances beyond my control that had the power to hurt her.

The game ended—our team lost—and Kendall arrived home about an hour later. "I'm so discouraged," she confessed with a quiver in her voice as she leaned against the kitchen counter. "Why did I have to sprain my ankle now?"

The question had no answer, of course, so I just put my arms around her, aching for the pain she felt. "You're tired now, and I don't blame you for feeling this way," I said after a minute. "But tomorrow will bring a whole new chance to try again."

She nodded and went off to her room to do some homework. A little later, I went in to say good night and found her in bed, flipping through her Bible. "I'm looking for a verse that jumps out and helps me," she said.

"Here's one of my favorite promises," I told her, turning to Jeremiah 29:11: " 'For I know the plans I have for you,' declares the LORD, 'plans to prosper you and not to harm you, plans to give you hope and a future.' "

She looked at those words a long time.

"Thanks, Mom," she said, snuggling down in her bed, the well-worn teddy bear of her childhood beside her.

I pulled the blankets up, kissed her forehead, and turned out the light.

As I walked down the hall, I realized that Kendall and I don't have many meaningful moments like that anymore. They seem to have mysteriously disappeared, just like the predictable dinner hour. But when they happen, I thank God for the reminder that I'm still part of this adolescent's security system in her up-and-down world—me and her Bible and her well-worn teddy bear.

Adolescence is a yo-yo time in the life of a family. Teenagers spin out and come reeling back in as they bounce between dependence and independence on their journey from childhood to adulthood. When the conditions feel smooth and nonthreatening, they confidently rush full speed ahead. But when the journey gets tough or discouraging, they limp back for a dose of love and encouragement. Sometimes they need hugs; sometimes they need to be left alone.

Sometimes they need structure and direction; sometimes they need the freedom to make their own decisions and even fail. Because of this yo-yoing, the journey seems confusing for both parents and adolescents. Each day has its ups and downs.

I weather the ups and downs better when I remember the task of adolescence is to *separate* and *gain independence;* to pull away and find an answer to the question "Who am I, apart from this family?" Separating is a normal and desirable part of growing up. We want our teens to begin showing signs of pulling away and gaining independence, yet those signs sometimes threaten our comfortable perception of family unity, which causes some friction.

Among the signs of separating that I've noticed at our house are assertiveness and rebellion, moodiness, and the need for privacy.

Assertiveness and Rebellion

One of the most obvious signs of separating is a new *assertiveness* that may appear to be *rebellion,* especially when it involves conflicts that turn into *control issues.* A son who's been fairly complacent, looking and thinking much like his dad, may suddenly start looking and acting differently in an attempt "to be me—instead of a little you." But he's still not sure who "me" is, and the process of finding out often means experimenting to discover who he is not. He may come home with a weird, new haircut or a little, gold earring. He may look as if he's rebelling, but sometimes, as an adolescent pulls away, the only way he can establish his own identity is to reject what his parents stand for. Maturity demands independence.

We have faced both the weird haircuts and the gold earring at our house. Weird haircuts were hard enough, but the earring was even harder.

Before he got his earring, Derek heard me glibly state that I didn't mind boys' wearing earrings. Many of his friends had experimented with the earring look, and I staunchly vowed that a small, gold loop in a boy's earlobe didn't change who he was or how I felt about him. But the Saturday afternoon Derek walked in the front door wearing an earring, I suddenly realized I meant this: I didn't mind earrings *in other boys' ears.* The sight of that earring in Derek's ear pushed some passionate, irrational buttons inside me. I started to take the whole thing personally, blowing it way out of proportion.

His earring means he doesn't like us, I decided, staring at that tiny, gold loop that glinted in the sun and nearly blinded me. *It's his way of rejecting all our values. And this is probably just the beginning. Next he'll dye his hair purple and orange, drop out of school, and quit going to church!*

"Oh, Derek," I moaned. "Why did you do that?"

"I just wanted to see what I look like," he said simply. Obviously, that seemed a perfectly logical and adequate reason to a 15-year-old.

"Ohhh," I moaned again. "I love you, Derek, but I don't like that earring." Even in my irrational state, a small voice somewhere reminded me to separate who Derek was from what he wore or did.

I knew that a conversation right then about the far-reaching ramifications of a boy wearing an earring would be useless. Besides, at that moment my intense emotions were blocking all rational responses. I needed to take time out to cool down and regain my perspective.

I don't want to oversimplify this cool-down period. My passionate responses to some parenting issues don't change easily or automatically with the passage of time. I usually have to go through several deliberate steps to reach a changed result, and those steps are hard work, because passionate issues like earrings (hairstyles, clothes, curfews, questionable friends) can turn into control issues, which are battlegrounds to avoid during our children's adolescence.

This is the question I ask myself: Has this turned into a control issue, which diverts attention from the real issue and centers instead on the question of "Who's in charge here?" A control issue usually means one person has to win (or be right) and one has to lose (or be wrong). A teenager seeking to separate and gain independence does not want to lose. And retaining total control is not my goal in dealing with an adolescent. My aim is to empower that adolescent by giving him some of the control that enables him to make his own decisions. So I try to clarify the conflict in my mind: Is this an issue about *who's in control* or an issue about *a boy wearing an earring?*

Then I ask myself some other questions: Why is this issue bothering me so much? Do I want him to change his appearance for *my* benefit (my need to know I'm still in control or to have him look a certain way) or for *his* (his need to gain some control over his appearance and to discover who he is)? Is this my problem or his? Is this issue morally threatening or life-threatening?

Furthermore, am I allowing him to express his opinion? Am I listening to him? He's searching for an answer to "Who am I?" and in the process, he wants to see if he likes the earring look. I don't like it on him. But we can have different tastes and opinions, and if we can learn to express them to each other with respect, we'll move a lot closer to a mature, adult relationship. We'll gain confidence in our ability to accept our differences and move beyond our disagreements. That's how healthy relationships grow and change through the seasons of life.

As I thought about these questions, my passion cooled. I prayed. I talked with Lynn, and I read a newspaper column by humorist Dave Barry about his son's getting his ear pierced. The episode made Dave feel he'd lost his ongoing battle to keep his son "normal, defined as 'like me.'"[1] He helped me realize my parental response is pretty universal, and so is the adolescent need to do something that parents wouldn't do, just to let us know they are not "like us."

Slowly, I put the earring issue into proper perspective. An earring isn't such a big deal. Big deals are things like honesty and integrity and the Ten Commandments, which are written in stone and represent the no-budge issues of our family. Wearing an earring is a relatively safe and harmless sign of separating, and the less we enter in on relatively safe issues, the less kids need to rebel to make their own statements.

In a few weeks, Derek quit wearing the earring, because he decided he didn't like it. That was an appropriate conclusion to the issue and far different from our telling him he couldn't wear it.

Some close families go through much more difficult periods of rebellion. As an encouragement to other families facing similar challenges, one mother and her 23-year-old son told their story of a journey through adolescent rebellion on the front page of our local newspaper. Living with this son through high school was like looking down a "long dark tunnel," according to the mom. At 15, he dropped out of school, ran away from home, and lived like a "punk," wearing army boots and black leather and indulging in drugs and alcohol. Though he moved back home twice during high school, he kept leaving, the last time because his parents told him to go in an expression of tough love. He spent Christmas Day that year riding a train to nowhere, and he remembers it as the most desolate time of his life.

Soon after that, he started an uphill battle to turn his life around, knowing his parents never gave up on him and always loved him. He got a job and began to accept responsibility. He got his general equivalency diploma (GED), and with his parents' help, he started college. Eventually, he graduated—Phi Beta Kappa. As both mother and son look back on those years, they agree they both had to grow and change. "I was part of the problem," the mom admits. "I had to see my son as an adult, not a child."

"But I wasn't acting like an adult," the son says. "I had to learn how the consequences of my actions not only affect me; they affect others, especially my mother."

"We never gave up," she explains. "We always believed the son we knew would emerge again. And he did."

Moodiness

A second sign of separating is *moodiness,* those unpredictable, up-and-down mood swings that are probably more common to adolescent girls than boys. But a teenager's down moods can infect a whole family. I've now lived through three teenage eras and can speak from experience. After a few slammed doors and silent treatments, I'm apt to take the rejection personally and feel like a failure as a parent.

The moodiness of adolescence may be brought on by hormonal changes and the ambivalence teenagers feel as they struggle to pull away from the people they've most depended upon. It's also brought on by the upheavals of their adolescent experiences. Teens want to appear tough and independent, yet they're actually pretty tender. Most of life's unfair realities are happening to them for the first time. The lessons that toughen them up are *tough* to live through.

"Mom," Kendall said as her voice broke into sobs over the phone one sunny Saturday afternoon, "I've been in a car accident."

Instantly, I got down to priorities. Was she hurt?

No, only badly shaken, but the car was crumpled. Then came the details. A woman ran a red light and rammed into Kendall, who was on her way home from taking care of a friend's dog. The woman got a ticket. Kendall got a smashed car—totaled, according to the insurance company. Unfortunately, its payment for the book value of the car wouldn't cover the cost of replacing it. "It's not fair," Kendall repeated over and over.

A few months later, I got another call from school. "Mom," Kendall said, sounding strangely quiet this time, "Gail was killed in a car accident today." She sounded as if she couldn't believe what she was saying. A friend, on her way to a volleyball tournament on icy roads, became an innocent victim. Sitting with Kendall late into that night, I tried to help her sort it out.

"When Gail woke up this morning, she had no idea this was her last day of life," Kendall said quietly, twisting a gum wrapper around her fingers. "It doesn't make *sense.*"

I nodded.

"But she lived her life right. Everybody liked her. She ended up right. I'll never forget her. But it still doesn't make sense."

Usually I see predictable patterns in our teens' moodiness. They're not morning people, so I tried to give them space in the morning. Later in the day, I would pose what they call my "interview questions": "What was the best thing about your day today?" "Did someone hurt your feelings today?" "Which was your hardest class today?"

I find it's easier to let a silent mood pass than try to change it. Sometimes separation is the best solution. If possible, I don't hang out too long around a moody teenager. And I tell myself that I'm not the cause of the moodiness, nor am I responsible to change it.

Some moodiness is expected, but being an adolescent should not become an excuse to be rude. Silence is one thing; talking back or sounding snippy is something much different. And moodiness is tolerable only if the "downs" are punctuated by some "ups." If "down" goes on too long, it's time to say enough is enough. Our teens tire of hearing a line that was passed down to me from my mother: "Learning to be pleasant—even when you don't feel like it—is one of life's great requirements."

They often rationalize a "down" period by telling me, "You just don't understand." I used to argue that point, hoping I'd convince them I do understand or try to understand, but I've given up. They like to believe I don't understand their moods or their problems, because that safely widens the gulf of separation they're seeking.

Need for Privacy

Another sign of separating is the *need for privacy.* Everyone knows that adolescence is a time when kids disappear into their bedrooms for long periods of time. They seek both physical and emotional space. They don't want us prying. I used to ask, "Who was that?" when they hung up the phone; it used to be a friendly question. Now it sounds like an invasion of their privacy.

Kendall hardly sees or talks to one friend anymore. "What happened?" I asked several times.

"Nothing," she kept repeating, which I know is not true, but she chose to keep the reasons to herself. She also may have chosen not to engage in any gossipy chatter with me, and I need to respect her desire for privacy in this matter, even though I sometimes feel left out of her personal life.

Again I remind myself that the need for privacy is a normal part of separating as teens seek to answer the question "Who am I?"

Paul Tournier, in his work *Secrets,* wrote, "Every human being needs secrecy in order to become himself and no longer a member of his tribe . . . in order to collect his thoughts. . . . To respect the secrecy of whoever it may be, even your own child, is to respect his individuality. To intrude upon his private life, to violate his secrecy, is to violate his individuality."[2]

The need for privacy often grows into a need to publicly pull away from the family, and an adolescent may begin to balk at accompanying the family on all outings. It may start out subtly, when the adolescent lags behind the family walking together across a restaurant parking lot because he or she doesn't want to look like the "nerdy Griswold family on vacation." An adolescent may sit by himself in the movie theater or with friends at church, or even beg off going out to eat with the family. Usually, these gestures are attempts to establish a sense of independence, and if accepted and allowed once in a while, they don't become patterns. They're part of the yo-yoing between dependence and independence.

These signs of separating—assertiveness and rebellion, moodiness, the need for privacy and pulling apart from the family—are tangible ways that adolescents remind us they're moving from childhood into adulthood. In a mothers' prayer group recently, we talked about our own yo-yo responses to these signs and how we feel about our kids' growing up and becoming more independent.

"It makes me feel *sad,*" one mother said. "Our family is changing and outgrowing some of our routines and traditions. I decorate the Christmas tree by myself now. We rarely sit together at church. They shop for clothes by themselves. As they become more independent, I'm losing a sense of companionship and responsibility I've enjoyed. It's difficult to let go of a good part of your life."

"I feel a little *afraid,*" another commented. "Will I be able to make this transition successfully? Will I be able to let go and become an observer instead of the controller? Once they are on their own, what will our family be like?"

"I also feel *excited,*" a third mother added. "I'm excited to see them growing up and testing their wings and showing their capabilities. I'm excited about the beginning of a new relationship."

"I'm all of the above," another stated. "Some days I know they're ready to move on, and so am I. I'm ready to give up night meetings at school, filling out registration papers, and being in charge of the master calendar. Then on other days, I get moody and scared and sad, just thinking about a nearly empty house."

These emotional responses show that as parents, we go through some of the same feelings our adolescents experience as we skitter back and forth between accepting and resisting these changes. The truth is, we raise our children to leave us, and sometimes that goal seems like a sad ending. Sometimes, however, it looks like a grand reward.

We, like them, yo-yo our way through this transition in life.

6

Choosing a College—Already?

"*W*hat do you want to be when you grow up?"
I remember how that question—usually posed to our young children by a grandmotherly person—flung open the doors to their dreams.

For Derek, the answer depended on the season and his outfit for the day—a fireman, professional football player, or famous basketball player.

Lindsay's or Kendall's fickle answer reflected the image of her current heroine—an ice-skater, television anchorwoman, or veterinarian.

But I remember how the meaning of that innocent question started changing about their junior year in high school, when teachers, counselors, our friends, and even their friends began asking the question for *real*.

"Have you given any thought to what you want to do when you grow up?" Derek's counselor asked him as we casually discussed a schedule change.

Derek's eyes widened as he realized it was not a grandmotherly question about childish dreams. He suddenly had no answer at all.

"I just want to be a high-school student for now," he moaned to me later.

Kids, like adults, get caught off guard with the realization that the years have passed so quickly, and suddenly it's time to make important decisions. The warning signals are flashing all around them. High school is a journey *toward* something, and starting in ninth grade, all courses and grades become part of a permanent record that follows them and counts toward post-high-school options like college.

"Everything starts counting now," we warned our teenagers as they entered high school, but we walk a tenuous line when we pass on that kind of advice. How do we encourage without pressuring or becoming parents who nag about grades and push our kids into certain activities because they would look good on a transcript and give them a better chance of getting into a prestigious college? Overpressuring means predetermining a student's post-high-school plans before that child even reaches high school. It means making choices *for* the child instead of *with* the child. I recently heard that an admissions officer at Harvard gets requests to talk to *kindergartners* about how to get into Harvard. That's pressuring!

Our role as parents is to encourage teens through a series of stressful and confusing choices so they can find a path that seems right for them at this point in their lives. In high school, that means determining areas of interest and ability in order to choose classes and think about options beyond high school. If college seems to be that option, as it is for nearly 60 percent of all high-school graduates, choices become even more important. Yet we assure them that few choices are irreversible. We change our minds; we change classes; we change majors; some people even change schools; and the average American adult changes jobs six times. Many kids are frightened that a choice made in tenth grade may affect them for the rest of their lives.

If it's the wrong choice, however, changes *are* possible.

The first step through the confusing choices is to take advantage of the tools schools offer. High-school counselors have been in the business of helping students through this stage of life longer than most parents. They offer good materials, but those materials are useless if they remain on the shelf (which is a possibility in our busy household, where lots of papers and letters come home from the schools).

One such resource is a workbook called *Now—High School . . . Then—What?* that's given to high schoolers in our area. It begins by asking the student some questions to determine interests and strengths: What are your patterns of choices as they have developed over the years in school, jobs, hobbies, or other activities? What's important to you? What bugs you? How much time do you spend studying? Do you enjoy learning? What are your most favorite and least favorite subjects in school? Imagine what you would like to be doing in five years, and rate the following: working; continuing your education; serving in the military; traveling. In ten years, how might you rank these in priority: money, home and family; health and friends?

The book encourages students to explore career possibilities by taking interest inventories or aptitude surveys, talking to people in different careers, volunteering in those areas, and attending career fairs.

Following several pages of questions and information, the student is asked to complete these sentences: "One idea I never realized about myself is _____"; and " One action I am going to take now to help me plan my future is_____."[1]

Post-High-School Options

In examining the various options available to high-school graduates, most teens need to choose one that involves additional training or schooling, because 80 percent of jobs now require it. Post-high-school options include the following:

Technical training. Many school districts have technical education centers that offer high-school and post-high-school programs to prepare students for entry-level employment in such fields as auto mechanics, computer operations and programming, cosmetology, graphic arts, practical nursing, and technical drafting.

On-the-job training. Some employers train new employees while they work in the areas of business, sales, secretarial service, and medical fields, to name a few.

Apprenticeship programs. Apprenticing is an earn-as-you-learn method of mastering highly complex trades in some major industries. It involves both on-the-job training and classroom instruction. Most employers register their apprenticeship opportunities through state apprenticeship councils. They include opportunities for firefighters, emergency medical technicians, legal secretaries, plumbers, painters, and welders.

Business, technical, and trade schools. Private schools provide training programs for a particular trade such as aeronautics and aerospace, accounting, forestry, health services, environmental control, cosmetology, court reporting, data processing, drafting, electronics, and mechanics. Classes last from a few months to a year or more.

Military service. Through programs in the U.S. Air Force, Army, Coast Guard, Navy, and Marine Corps, high-school graduates receive on-the-job training for many occupational specialties. In a four-year enlistment, a person can receive the equivalent of a junior college education in fields such as business administration, electronic communications, medical technology, computer technology, police science, and physical therapy, as well as many others. In areas such as engineering and nursing, the military will send a person through four or more years of college in exchange for an extended period of enlistment.

Community colleges. Two-year colleges offer occupational programs for students wanting specialized training, and also transfer programs for those wanting to continue their training at a four-year college. Public community colleges are generally the least-expensive way to go to college.

Four-year colleges. High-school graduates choosing four-year colleges face many related choices: size, location, major courses, cost, and facilities, to name a few. Because the majority of high-school graduates go on to college, we will examine some of those related choices and the application process, which surprises many students.

As one high-school senior confessed, "I never thought the experience would be so stressful and difficult—filling out all those forms and essay questions, making decisions, waiting and fearing rejection."

As a parent, I didn't know, either. But now that we've been through the process twice and are about to start our third round, we've learned some tips and gathered lots of information. Collecting information is one way we can lessen the burden of responsibility on bewildered high-school students who suddenly find themselves plunked down in the middle of a countdown toward college while also struggling to keep up with the obligations of high school. The first thing we did was invest in a couple of books about choosing a college. Counseling offices and libraries offer some; many are annual publications that describe and rate schools, such as *U. S. News & World Report's Annual Guide to America's Best Colleges,* the yearly edition of *Best Buys in College Education,* or one in the series of Peterson's Guides called *Choose a Christian College.*

Parents' Role in Choosing a College

Give students a choice. As the parents' first step, define your role in helping your son or daughter determine the choice of a college.

Instead of predetermining that choice or making it for the student, the best things we can do are to gather and give information, identify and state our boundaries or limitations to those choices, and then offer encouragement and support as that choice is made. We prayed our high-school seniors would be accepted by at least two colleges that were acceptable to us so the final choice was theirs. At that stage of their growing independence, they need to have ownership of the decision. Otherwise, they won't buy into it with the same sense of personal commitment.

I've known parents who predetermine that a certain prestigious college is the only right choice, as if acceptance to a highly competitive school will become an *A* on their report card of parenting. They don the sweatshirt of that school or proudly plaster decals on the back of the family car. As parents, we define the goal of our role—to help our sons and daughters find a school (or other post-high-school choice) that's right for them. The best college is the one that's best for them. We don't want to set them up for failure by pressuring them into choices that aren't right for them; we want to help them succeed in a college that matches their abilities and meets their needs.

Gather and file information. The amount of information that begins to accumulate regarding college choices and applications quickly overwhelms a high-school student. At our house, we felt we might drown in a sea of paper, so we offered to bring order to the chaos, and our students gladly accepted the help.

We first set up a system. Lynn is the superorganizer in our family, so he got a sturdy, portable file box with folders and started keeping all the information together, but in separate files. The student time line (see chart at the end of this chapter) proved invaluable, because we could keep track of the necessary steps along the way. We taped that to the top of the box and also kept a calendar handy, marking necessary dates and deadlines for tests, letters, and applications. With this system, we rarely lost papers or missed a deadline.

In addition to keeping track of information, we gathered helpful advice by talking with counselors, teachers, and other parents. In fact, parenting a child through this stage of life reminded me of parenting an infant through the baby stage. All that talk about feeding and burping seemed deathly boring and unimportant before we had a baby. Then we had a child, and those conversations suddenly became fascinating. The same is true with conversations about leaving home and choosing colleges. It all seemed so boring a few years ago, but suddenly, we felt magnetically drawn to those conversations as we shared information and encouragement with other parents. "How is the SAT different from the ACT?" we asked each other. "What do you know about John Brown University? How do we know if we qualify for financial aid?"

Offer advice. Because we gathered information, we could pass on helpful advice in the areas where our teens were willing to accept it. For instance, we learned that colleges don't want well-rounded students; they want well-rounded classes made up of lop-sided students who excel in one or two areas. Most colleges believe that consistently good grades in quality courses are still the best indicators of potential in college; and they especially dislike the choice of "Mickey Mouse" courses the senior year. We offered advice on how to fill out an application so that it stands out, how to know if an SAT refresher course is worthwhile, and assorted other tidbits.

Determine and state limits to the choice. If we want our students to make the final choice, we need to define our boundaries or limitations early in the process. For each family, those boundaries will be different. Lynn and I recognized that finding a good college that met the needs of our children for their first year away from home was a high priority and wise investment. We vowed that we would do all we could within our budget to send them to the school that seemed right for them—with a few limitations. We based those limitations on our knowledge of our children—their personalities, strengths, and needs:

Small schools. We believe our children need the nurturing, individual attention, and personal challenge found in smaller classes and dormitories at smaller schools, ideally 5,000 students or less. Though some students thrive amidst the stimulation of a large university, we wanted a place where our children were less likely to slip through the cracks, at least for their first year away from home. Both Lynn and I attended large universities where we found ourselves in some classes with 500 other people. Nobody knew if we missed the class; worse, nobody cared. Smaller classes provide an opportunity to know professors personally and to write essay answers to tests (rather than true/false or multiple choice), which teaches students to express themselves and develop their critical thinking skills.

Liberal arts. Neither of our older children went through high school with a passionate, clear leaning toward a specific career or field of interest, so we believed a liberal arts college would best prepare them to become competent, knowledgeable, disciplined people who can write and speak effectively, work well with people, and think critically within any chosen field. We believe a liberal arts curriculum educates for life, not just a specific job.

Christian or non-Christian. I include this as an important consideration, though we didn't make it a strict limitation, and I'll discuss the differences in more detail later. For the first year away from home, we believe that a Christian school offers the most-nurturing environment and a proper balance between academic excellence and Christian commitment. But we also believe that when it comes to matters of faith, an 18-year-old faces *choices,* not *requirements.* We offered our opinions and information, but we didn't limit their choice to a Christian school.

Geographical location. If our teens desired to go away from home or out of state, we encouraged that choice. We believe, if they are ready, that geographical distance increases their potential to gain independence. If they don't make that adjustment to leaving home now, they'll have to make it at some later date. We pointed out the subtle influences of growing up in Colorado, such as *climate* (Colorado has a mild climate and majority of sunny days), *urban or rural area* (Boulder is close to Denver, therefore not a rural or isolated area), and the fact they grew up in the shadow of a large state university (Boulder is home to the University of Colorado, which has its own little town area called "the Hill" and major spectator sports events like football and basketball).

Cost and budget. Our children know the total budget allotted for their four years of school. Beyond that, they have to share the responsibility of finding financial aid. The fact is, many of the more expensive private institutions offer more financial aid than public institutions, so don't rule them out without investigating first. For instance, we checked into several small, liberal arts, Christian colleges which claim that up to 70 percent of their students receive financial aid in the form of scholarships, grants, loans, and work-study jobs.

Our main goal in setting limitations fits that old axiom of parenting: When giving choices, whether it's what to wear or where to eat lunch, give only those options you're willing to live with. In helping them select a college, we want to open the door to several choices and leave it open wider than the father who gave his son a list of schools to choose from—and there was only one school on the list. "I've looked into it, and I'm convinced this is the best bargain in higher education today," the father rationalized. I pray the son shares the father's enthusiasm through his first year away at college.

Student's Role in Choosing a College

Within those limitations, our teenagers began the arduous project of listing and then narrowing their possible choices. Obviously, our limitations immediately trimmed their choices. So did the descriptions we found in books and magazine articles available through the high-school counseling office, various school catalogues, and even a growing supply of videos. Colleges were also added and dropped based on personal recommendations (knowing someone who goes to a certain school helps in getting honest answers to real questions!), college representatives visiting the high schools, and visits to the campuses.

For some time, we'd been stopping at college campuses along every vacation route, and during our teens' high-school years, at least one spring vacation was planned specifically to visit college campuses. Visits that are made when school is in session and students are on campus give an honest taste of the school's personality. When the list is down to six or less, the criteria become more specific. We checked and rechecked the following:

Academic quality. What are the core curriculum requirements? What courses do they emphasize? What makes their curriculum different from that of similar schools? What opportunities beyond the classroom are offered? How many distinguished members of the faculty teach undergraduate courses? What is the average class size? What provisions do they make for academic advising? How much personal help do students get in making out their schedules and getting admitted into classes during registration?

Room, board, and tuition costs, and financial aid available.

Facilities. What are the library, laboratories, classrooms, and dormitories like?

Extracurricular activities. What sports, volunteer, and leadership opportunities are available?

Personality of the school. This more nebulous quality is best judged by visiting the campus. Fitting in is more important than getting in, and visiting a class, eating in the dining hall, talking with other students, and even staying overnight in a dorm help determine whether a student would feel comfortable.

Christian or non-Christian school. Our two high-school seniors had both Christian and non-Christian schools on their final lists. The choice was theirs, but these are some issues we discussed and questions we asked a dean of students and president of a Christian college.

Why choose a Christian school over a non-Christian school?
"If you give me your children for only one year of their lives, give me their freshman year—their first year away from home—when they are most vulnerable and impressionable, bombarded with choices and trying to develop views about life and values and truth and who they are. Let me surround them with some Christian mentors and role models during this tough time of transition."

How does the teaching style differ at Christian and non-Christian schools?
"On most secular campuses, there's an attitude of moral, cultural, and ethical relativity. This view says it is impossible to know what is true because all truth is relative, and truth is whatever you believe it to be. It is not 'politically correct' to believe in the Bible's absolute truth. It takes a strong Christian to flourish and grow in this environment, but some do and come out stronger for it."

Does a Christian school prepare students for life in the real world, or is it too narrow and protective?
"Some are too narrow, depending upon how much freedom they give their students to make personal decisions and whether they teach them to critically examine all sides of controversial issues. A Christian college, worthy of the name of Christ, must be scrupulously honest in its search for truth, admit problems that exist, and present alternatives with respect. We try to teach our students to live *in* the world but not be *of* the world. We encourage them to care passionately about the truth and develop critical thinking skills so they can separate the valid from the invalid, strong arguments from weak arguments, and truth from error. We teach them that their Christian faith is relevant to all of life, and they can apply their faith to the issues they face in college and in the real world after graduation. While they're on campus, we treat our students as young adults; we don't

merely want to protect them from the world for four years. We believe that overprotection often leads to rebellion or rejection of their faith."

What Colleges Look for in a Student

Choosing a college is a two-way process; the student chooses the college, but the college also chooses the student. That's part of the good match. "What are colleges looking for these days?" we asked as we got involved in the college search process. Here's what we found out.

Grades. Good grades in quality courses, beginning with the freshman year, remain the most important factor on a transcript and the best indicator of whether a student will succeed in college. "We want to admit students who will graduate," one admissions counselor said. Good course selection throughout the four years of high school, including classes in physics, chemistry, English, and history (especially advanced placement), indicates that students like to challenge themselves. Grade trends matter, too. An upward trend helps; a declining trend hurts.

Test scores. Test scores are not as vital as good grades. High test scores but low grades indicate laziness or lack of motivation, and high grades can offset poorer test scores, especially because schools recognize that some people are not good test takers. Students might consider taking an SAT or ACT refresher course if their practice test scores were low; if they had trouble finishing in time or difficulty remembering junior high math, especially ratios, fractions, and percentages; if they had trouble on the verbal, grammar, and reading comprehension parts of the practice test; or if they suffer from test anxiety or lack basic test-taking strategies. Most counseling offices have a booklet called "Preparing for the SAT" that offers test-taking tips.

Extracurricular activities. Admissions people look for students who do more than study. Leadership in one area is better than participation in many. A student does well to pick one activity or skill, stick with it, and excel in it. The same is true with sports. We feared Derek had narrowed himself in basketball through high school, but an admissions counselor told us they liked the fact that he not only played that varsity sport for three years, but he also volunteered at summer basketball camps, helping inner-city children learn the skills.

Admissions officers are not impressed with parent-purchased, one-shot summer experiences such as trips to Europe. They prefer follow-through in ongoing projects like working in the local soup kitchen, especially when that activity shows the student reaches beyond himself or herself to help someone else. They like unusual activities: If a student plays an instrument, the oboe stands out more than the trumpet.

Faculty recommendations. Praise and information need to be specific to make a difference. Assist faculty members with these letters by giving them plenty of time and personal information. Some high-school counseling offices ask a student to fill out forms to give faculty members so they can write specific letters. Recommendation letters also help explain a sudden plunge in grades or a discrepancy between grades and test scores.

Application forms and essays. At a college-night gathering in our area, I saw a young man stop by a table, pick up an application, and start filling it out in pencil. "Take it home and take your time," an admissions director gently advised. The message is: Neatness counts. So do thoroughness, thoughtfulness, and timeliness. The applications consist of several parts: lengthy forms requiring personal information, such as a list of all schools attended, and a series of essay questions ("Describe a turning point in your life" or "You have just written a 300-page autobiography; send us page 258"). Answers to essay questions vary in importance from school to school, but they're intended to reflect thinking and writing skills, creativity, and personality. They give the student a chance to "talk" to the admissions people. In an effort to stand out, some students send videos, pieces of original artwork (including a pair of tennis shoes painted with "I'm running to get into C.U."), even a 45 rpm rock 'n' roll recording.

Other. Colleges look for students with a combination of academic achievement, intellectual curiosity, commitment, communication abilities, personality, and initiative. One admissions director at a Christian school said she also looks for "red flags," or problems that might hinder a student's success at college: "A recent death in the family or divorce or eating disorder or past discipline problem does not mean a student isn't college material, but we ask whether the time is right. The transition of leaving home causes tremendous upheaval, and when compounded with other problems, the adjustment may be too much. We want kids to succeed."

Other students go through the admissions process but begin to fear they aren't ready for college, so they decide to take a year off. "I need to get the 'ya-yas' out of my system," one student said. Whatever that means, parents need to discern, sometimes with the help of a counselor, whether the student is experiencing the normal precollege jitters or an honest desire to gain a year of maturity before going to college.

"I recommend several options to students considering a year off, and I know those same students will come to college stronger and more motivated a year later," this admissions director said. Options include one-year programs through Christian organizations such as Youth With A Mission (YWAM), Capernwray Bible Schools, or any number of opportunities advertised in Christian magazines. Students might work, travel, or check into the "Transition to College" program through the National Association of Independent Schools in Boston (phone 617- 451-2444), which offers various one-year boarding-school plans around the United States.

Sending Off the Applications

Completing the applications on time can be a struggle, like a sprint for the finish line or, rather, the deadline. Many families find it a stressful time when parents nag and students procrastinate. We know we're supposed to let our seniors "own their own problems" and therefore the consequences, but when the door to a major opportunity is clanging closed because of a missed deadline, that seems too big a consequence for some parents to let go of. So there's tension.

One mother finally gave up after days of reminding her son of the approaching deadline. "This is now your responsibility," she told him. "I will say nothing more." The night before the deadline, he stayed up late, writing out his essays on the computer. The next morning he left, the completed application in hand, but the answers were still on the screen. The mother read them and cringed. The writing was good, but she spotted glaring errors in grammar and spelling. The consequence was his. He was not accepted into that school—but he was accepted into another, where he is now happy. "It's probably a better match," the mother concluded a year later.

No matter how we reach it, the day finally comes when the applications are complete. I remember the feeling at our house—a mixture of great relief and new anxiety for our kids: "What if I get rejected? Have I done the best I can on the applications? How do I endure the waiting?"

The answers for us came in another prayerful trip up Mount Moriah to a place of surrender. Before we put those applications in the mail, we said a prayer of relinquishment. We acknowledged to God that we'd done the best we could—surely not perfect, but a dedicated effort—and now we trusted the opened or closed doors to be part of His grand plan. We dropped them in the mailbox, and the metal door clanged closed. They were out of our hands—and in His. "Do the possible and trust God to do the impossible," I once heard.

Most schools let you know when to expect an answer, and around that time, the student comes home every day asking, "Any mail? Did we hear?" The famous advice is to hope for a fat envelope rather than a thin one. Thin ones contain a single-page letter of rejection. Fat ones contain official forms and welcoming information. Odds are, if young people apply to several schools, they're bound to get at least one rejection, and rejections are plain tough.

How can we help? By sharing their disappointment and allowing them to grieve rather than trying to talk them out of their feelings. "I'm disappointed for you" or "I know how much this means to you," we tell them. Time helps. So do the acceptances from other schools. In our own minds, we have to trust that the acceptance/rejection process keeps our kids out of the schools that would not be right for them.

More than one acceptance assures that the final choice is up to the student, an answer to prayer in our case. Our two were accepted by both Christian and non-Christian schools. One seemed clear on a choice; the other struggled a bit more. "How do you know God's will?" the teenager asked.

"If it doesn't seem clear, He may care more about the heart attitude you carry off to college than the name of the college," we said.

In the end, one chose a Christian college, while the other chose a non-Christian school. In retrospect (because God's will always seems clearer in hindsight), they both appear to be at the schools that are right for them and on the path of growth divinely designed to meet their needs. Both have felt nurtured by their small-school environments, and both seem challenged. (Admittedly, though, the one attending a non-Christian school faces greater adversity and is forced to answer some tough questions, but that student has also found Christian support within various small groups and is stretching toward great growth.)

As I look back, I'm convinced that students could be happy at several different schools and in many different post-high-school experiences. Though the decision is important and profoundly shapes the future of the high-school graduate, when we surrender ourselves to God, He weaves all our circumstances together for good.

~Student's College Planning Time Line~

Sophomore Year

October: Some sophomores take the PACT or PSAT, practice versions of the ACT and SAT exams taken in the junior and senior years. Practice exams help you determine if you want to take a refresher course and give you an assessment of your academic skills. Results are not passed along to colleges.

Junior Year

September: Attend college fairs in your area, where representatives from hundreds of schools hand out information and answer questions. You should also register for the PSAT, even if you took it as a sophomore.

October: Take the PSAT.

December: Review PSAT scores with your guidance counselor. Using scores as one factor, discuss the type of school you might attend. Check schedules, and determine when you will take the ACT or SAT and achievement tests that measure knowledge in specific areas. Registration for each test is about six weeks in advance. Determine which schools will receive your test results.

January to March: Develop a preliminary list of 10 to 12 colleges that sound interesting. Start collecting information from those schools, noting deadlines, tests, and information required for admission. Next fall's early decision candidates must take the SAT and achievement tests before June. Review your senior year course plan to make sure you are completing all academic courses required by the colleges in which you are interested.

Spring break: Visit college campuses, if possible, noticing the differences between large and small, rural and urban schools. Seek to identify the personality of schools. Visit classes, eat in the cafeteria, talk with students, and stay in a dormitory.

May: Take advanced placement tests if you qualify. High scorers receive college credits.

Summer: Plan additional campus visits, if possible. Schedule formal interviews on any campus where you plan to seek an early decision (which usually commits you to attend that school if you're accepted).

Senior Year

September: Narrow your list of schools to a manageable number (four to six) to which you will make formal application. Obtain application forms; check dates, tests, and deadlines for those schools. Line up teachers to write the recommendations that will accompany your applications. Start thinking about your essays. If you are applying under any early decision plans, make sure your transcript is ready to go.

October: Send applications to any schools with rolling admissions (acceptances as they are received).

November: Send early decision applications. Take the SAT again.

December: Pick up financial aid forms from the guidance office, and file them. Complete and send in applications. Early decision responses will arrive from about December 15 to December 31.

January: Last chance to take the SAT and achievement tests for the fall freshman class. Final deadlines for most applications are between January 15 and March 1. Have your high-school counseling office send transcripts of your first-semester grades to colleges to which you've applied.

March and April: Acceptance and rejection letters are sent. Continue to do your best work in school; colleges check for signs of senioritis. Inform your counseling office which school you decide to attend so it will mail your final transcript.

7

Senioritis and a Mid-life Crisis

"Senioritis is a common, though rarely fatal, disease," a high-school counselor and friend explained with a smile as we sat in her office discussing graduation, leaving home, and family transitions. "Literally, it means a 'flu of the personality' or 'inflammation of the senior,' though the disease sometimes dips down and strikes younger students. Symptoms include irritability, irresponsibility, and lack of enthusiasm. The afflicted are not easy to love, yet they greatly need our love and understanding. Though their behavior may seem like the problem, it's only a symptom. The problem is their fear of growing up, facing changes, and the impending loss of childhood."

Fear of facing changes and impending losses—sounds a lot like the emotions of mid-life, I mused.

As teenagers make the transition between childhood and adulthood, they feel confused. In one moment, they look forward to finishing high school, but in the next, they feel frightened. Graduation marks the official end of childhood and threatens to end the structured, predictable way of life they've known for the last 18 years. It means losing a huge chunk of security while facing a future that looks exciting but insecure. As they get closer to graduation, they may act out their fears in various forms of negative behavior that they don't even understand, because adolescents are not good at identifying and verbalizing their fear of losses.

Judith Viorst, in *Necessary Losses,* explained those fears and the need to grieve their losses—especially the loss of family—this way:

> This separation—this loss of the closest attachments of our life—is often frightening and always sad. The gates of Eden are clanging shut for good. And to this add the loss of our self-as-child and the loss of our former familiar body and the loss of our fuzzy innocence as we tune into the tough truths on the evening news. As with every important loss we need to mourn—we need to mourn our childhood's end—before we can be emotionally free to commit to love and to work in the human community. . . . Adolescents, in this letting-go stage of life, experience "an intensity of grief unknown in previous phases."[1]

"How can we help them through this transition?" I asked my friend. She offered two suggestions. First, we can think about growing up from their point of view, remembering our own feelings and fears during adolescence, which will increase our patience and understanding of their negative or moody behavior. Second, we can encourage them to recognize, acknowledge, and grieve their impending losses, which might help them move on to the next stage of life more smoothly.

In taking the first step, I challenged myself to consider their losses as I set out on a walk the next afternoon. I imagined being a senior, anticipating the thought of leaving home in a few months, and I imagined several kinds of loss.

Naming Their Losses

First, there is the *loss of childhood,* which means the loss of protection, innocence, and a more carefree way of life. There's the *loss of security* and *predictability* within the context of a familiar life pattern; and there's the *loss of place* within the family (being the older brother or oldest child). There's the *physical loss of home*, which includes the loss of a bedroom and its privacy, the loss of access to a car, and the loss of a refrigerator and cupboard stocked by someone else.

Then there's the *loss of a high-school class* that, for years, carefully wove itself together through shared experiences like football victories, grief over the death of a classmate in a car accident, and the common responses to the quirks of a principal or popular teacher. Though some class members will gather for reunions in the future, graduation means this class will cease to exist as a unit moving together through time.

Within the larger class is a smaller, more intimate *circle of friends*, and the senior faces the loss of a place within that carefully constructed group. It's a body built around both differences and similarities, but the bond is strong, because the group has a history and has endured the test of time. The friends don't have to explain to each other that one is a good basketball player, diabetic, from a single-parent family, brilliant, or afraid of flying, because they all know that stuff. There is great comfort in knowing and being known, and great grief in losing the sense of belonging to such a close-knit group.

There's even the *loss of accountability and guidance* as the senior begins to cope with the fact that "the person in charge of me is me!" It shouldn't be surprising that seniors who are trying to separate from their caretakers act out their mixed-up feelings in so many confusing ways. From their viewpoint, their carefully constructed world is crumbling apart.

No wonder Peter Pan vowed, "I won't grow up!"

I came home from my walk that day sensitized to the senior's point of view and hoping to open some nonthreatening discussions about *feelings* at our house. Timing is important with such discussions. Sometimes during that spring before graduation, Derek seemed like a sleep-and-eat machine, silently moving through the house as if he needed to detach himself from personal involvement. Other times, he lingered at the kitchen counter as if he wanted to talk. That's when I posed some questions.

"Does it sometimes feel scary to think about leaving all your friends and moving out of your room here? What's the best part of being a senior? What's the hardest part? What can we do to help?" I asked.

"The best part about being a senior is knowing I'm almost done with high school," he said, "but that's also the hardest part." And then he told me about a recent experience. Driving home from school one day, he heard a song on the radio that reminded him of autumn, always his favorite time of year. But he suddenly realized how totally different and unfamiliar the next fall would feel. "I got this pain in my stomach and thought I'd have to pull over because I felt sick," he said.

"Give your child roots and wings," the old saying goes. But for the adolescent on the brink of leaving home, the roots do battle with the wings. In *Passages,* Gail Sheehy referred to two forces living within each person, a "Merger Self" and a "Seeker Self." The Merger Self gives us the impulse to attach ourselves to others, especially parents and family when we're young. The Seeker Self is the opposite impulse that drives us to seek individuality, to be separate and pursue our own destinies. Sheehy explained, "These impulses are driven by contradictory wishes that set up the push-pull underlying all steps of development."[2]

Acting Out Their Losses

How do adolescents act out those confusing push-pull feelings? Some get lazy and quit doing homework or start cutting classes. For those students, senioritis or the senior slump means a sudden lack of effort toward any academic pursuit. Many excellent students act that way and claim the letdown is justified after years of feeling pressured to earn good grades to get into college. Now that their college applications are completed, they decide to take it easy. High-school counselors believe some seniors even subconsciously sabotage their ability to graduate by cutting classes and avoiding homework, because failure will bring a last-minute reprieve from the challenge of moving on and facing the losses graduation brings.

Other seniors head to the counseling office for help in resolving issues with friends or parents. They want to deal with unfinished business before it's too late.

Some seem irritable or sullenly silent, especially at home. Though they can't define or admit it, this behavior often covers up their fear of impending loss. The honest message is, "It will be easier for me to leave this family if I act as though I don't like you."

The movie *Terms of Endearment* contains a poignant example of this behavior in a scene where the young mother who is dying of cancer calls her two children to her hospital room for her last good-bye. Courageously, she begins her difficult message. The younger one, probably in grade school, honestly acts out his feelings and cries as she talks. But the other, an adolescent, responds totally differently, acting cool and even cruel, as if he doesn't care or doesn't like her. She accepts his behavior with patient understanding, and as well as I can recall, she tells him, "In the future, when you remember our time together today, I want you to know that I understand why you're acting this way—and I love you."

What a tender example of a mother who forgives her son because she knows that acting angry is the only way he can cope with saying good-bye! Selflessly, she helps him through that painful moment for both of them.

It will be easier for me to say good-bye if I act as though I don't like you. That rationalization, no matter how mixed up it comes out, masks lots of behavior as an adolescent thinks about leaving home. The butterfly, just before emerging from the cocoon, goes through a tremendous struggle to unfurl its wings. In childbirth, the pain of that final struggle precedes and enables the delivery, or new beginning.

Parents can help teenagers through this difficult transition by encouraging them to identify and acknowledge their feelings whenever possible. After I started asking those questions about fears, my kids and I began talking about their normal feelings and responses. We identified and even named the silences and periods of irritability, using the code words "detach mode" and "senior syndrome." Somehow this small gesture said, "I understand your feelings."

Parents can also help by responding with patience and not taking adolescents' negative behavior personally. We should not assume their moody silences mean they don't like us. Usually, the opposite is true. That behavior is the only way they can cope with their fears about leaving home.

The irony is that we parents face similar fears of losses as our seniors prepare to leave home. We fear their leaving will forever change the family structure, our definitions of ourselves, and our parental job descriptions. The anticipation of their leaving often coincides with—or precipitates—the feelings connected with mid-life transitions. We, too, face an uncertain future.

When these separate but similar fears about losses meet on the same stage, one of two things can happen. We can have honest, openhearted discussions or openly heated exchanges of angry words that neither individual means and are almost always regretted later. We hope for the openhearted discussions, which are more apt to happen when we adults can openly identify our feelings. And that begins for us just as it does for them—with a better look at our anticipated losses.

Naming Our Losses

Here are some of my anticipated losses:

Loss of being needed. In some ways, there's a liberation associated with this loss, but a nostalgic part of me remembers how nice it felt to be needed. My face used to be the only one that could stop my child's crying in the church nursery, but now that same child calls her friend when she wants comfort and understanding. She doesn't need me to fix her moods anymore, but I still relish those brief moments when I'm needed, such as when she doesn't feel good and crawls into our bed in the middle of the afternoon. I sit beside her, rub her back, bring her some juice, and enjoy the privilege of taking care of her. (I'll probably enjoy it for the rest of my life, especially as those opportunities decrease.)

Loss of identity. Inevitably, people are defined by their titles—mother, daughter, wife, sister, accountant, doctor—because most titles also carry built-in job descriptions. I realize that *mother* means something far different today, as our children leave home, from what it meant when they were little. I no longer tell the barber how to cut my son's hair. My daughter doesn't ask my permission to visit a friend. I've lost the role of being in charge. I face other connected losses, too, such as the loss of involvement in their activities and connection to their friends. Those teenagers who watched movies in our family room and raided our refrigerator no longer show up or call. Though that may sound liberating, I name it as a loss. I genuinely care about those kids and their lives.

Loss of clear priorities and excuses. Family has been my top priority for the last 20 years. Though I worked part-time while our children were growing up, I've had clear boundaries that served as my protective shield. "No, I can't do that weekend workshop because of my family," I've said many times, and that reasoning is usually respected. As my kids leave home, I can't use that rationalization. I've run out of excuses. Erma Bombeck described a similar fear when she put her baby on the bus to kindergarten and faced an empty home. "My excuse for everything just got on that bus. . . . These walls have been so safe for the last few years. I didn't have to prove anything to anyone. Now I feel vulnerable. What if I apply for a job and no one wants me? What if I can't let go of my past?"[3]

That last question haunts me, too, when I think about losses. Surely it's time to move on, and part of me looks forward to that, but the past also holds me powerfully in its grip. I caught a glimpse of this while viewing home movies at my brother's house. I sat transfixed as I watched myself chatting with an assortment of relatives on his back porch one summer afternoon, while our kids kept parading through, squealing and giggling. What stunned me (in addition to how much younger I looked) was how animated and absorbed I seemed by my children as I scooped them up and answered their endless questions. *Will I ever feel that fulfilled again?* I wondered. *Will the next chapter of my life bring that same kind of joy? How much of who I am is tangled up with who they are?* The pull of the past gave me an uneasy uncertainty about the future as I wondered who I would be on the other side of this transition.

Those questions about changes and identity at mid-life are similar to the questions high school seniors ask themselves. I remember a time in Lindsay's senior year when I realized how closely my feelings matched hers—and how she unwittingly showed me a way of coping. As she filled out her college applications, she feared an uncertain future away from home, and I feared an uncertain future at home without her, my second child and first daughter, who was an important part of my daily life.

One Saturday morning in early January, she sat at the kitchen counter, staring at three college applications. She had filled out the specific information, like class rank and grade schools attended, but she was stuck on the tough essay section, where the creative answers are supposed to contain revealing information that will help the school decide if the applicant is worthy of being admitted.

"I can't do this!" she wailed as she dropped her pencil on the stack of forms. "I'm supposed to tell them who I am and what I want to become, *and I don't know!*" Her eyes filled with tears as she looked at me pleadingly.

I'd already seen those essay items: (1) Choose one adjective that describes yourself and tell us why. (2) In 20 years, you're given a prestigious community award. What is it for, and why were you selected? (3) Write a short autobiography, showing the development of your strengths.

I cringed in sympathy because I'd have a hard time knowing how to respond myself, but also because I felt instinctively protective and angry at a system that demanded that kind of self-examination at such an insecure time in a teenager's life. At the moment when Lindsay felt most confused about who she was, she had to come up with answers to those probing questions. It seemed unfair and impossible. Surely, this struggle would shake her already fragile sense of self-confidence even more. I put my arm around her.

"Why don't you take a rest and work on this later?" I suggested, knowing her frustration would keep her from writing good answers.

A couple of weeks and many hard-working sessions later, Lindsay completed her applications, and she appeared almost transformed by the process. She seemed more confident, which I assumed came from the relief of finishing the project. But when I read one of her cover letters, I discovered a different reason.

"Thank you for the opportunity to answer these tough questions," she wrote. "They helped me reach a clearer definition of myself."

I stood staring at those words, again learning a lesson in parenting that I seem to keep forgetting. Instinctively, I wanted to protect Lindsay from the struggle of coming up with those answers, but my sympathy almost got in the way of her growth, because she found *strength* in the struggle. She also discovered a *solution* in the struggle. She had to dig into her past and identify the threads of her personality that helped her clarify her hopes for the future.

She realized she'd always been a people person from the time her preschool teacher nicknamed her "head girl of the class." She usually championed the cause of the underdog, even trying to rescue a field mouse from her cat at about age six, and patiently working with a skittish horse in 4-H. Her family and faith had always been foundational priorities, and as she looked back over the tapestry of threads, she realized they formed a pattern that pointed to her future; she wanted to study sociology and become a family counselor or social worker, possibly helping abused children.

Lindsay's lack of confidence came partly from her lack of a clear answer to the "Who am I?" question. But when she took the time to examine her past, she found specific examples that helped her form some answers and feel more secure about her future.

The same holds true for me. In facing my insecurities or confusion about entering a different season, I must do more than merely ask the question, Who do I want to be on the other side of this transition? Like Lindsay, I have to struggle all the way through to some answers by identifying the passions in my past that might clarify what I want to do with my future.

While our kids were young, I felt privileged to stay at home with them, where I worked part-time as a free-lance writer, mostly on the subject of family. During those early years, I often got up at 5:00 A.M. to find quiet spaces of time. When the children got older, I increased my workload, filling in the growing gaps of free time with more jobs. But now, as I near the end of my active parenting role, I'm no longer *needed* at home, and I face more choices. As I examine my past, however, I realize my passion still centers on family-oriented issues, and though I may change the location of my work, I want to remain within that subject area.

Change—the Common Denominator

There's one common denominator in seeking new answers to the "Who am I?" question and facing the choices in a major transition.

It's common to Lindsay's transition from high school and mine at mid-life. It's called *change*. As C. S. Lewis said, "To live in time is to change, because time is change." Change in life is inevitable; change is healthy; and change is a natural by-product of the Christian's earthly pilgrimage. Coping with change demands two steps: being *willing* to change and *preparing* to change.

In her book *Turning Points,* which describes the process of personal change, Ellen Goodman talked about "change resisters" and "change innovators." In facing transitions, both seek ways to conserve meaning in their lives while avoiding a sense of loss. Change resisters do it by avoiding change at all costs, because they see change as threatening rather than hopeful or exciting. They value safety and sameness and hold on to traditions and patterns of the past. They tend to be worriers, always warning others to watch out or be careful. They get stuck in the past, which keeps them from seeing the potential in the future. I've known parents like that in mid-life. They don't let go of the way things were, and their grown children don't want to visit them because they're still treated like children.

I fear I could become a parent like that unless I'm *willing* to change.

Change innovators, on the other hand, leap into radical change, denying the importance of any traditions or commitments. They often take dramatic shortcuts into the future, wholeheartedly determined to make a fresh start to a new way of life. I've also known people like that at mid-life; they've suddenly "had enough" and walked out on their marriages or families, leaving broken people in their wake, as if they don't even notice or care.

Goodman also described a third alternative, however, called the "middle ground-ers," which means being *willing* to change but in a timely pattern, considering the needs and circumstances of significant others. Middle ground-ers identify and keep the traditional values of the past while looking forward to the change and growth of the future.[4]

In describing these three patterns of response, Goodman also defined the trends of contemporary society that affect the changes and remind me that our children are growing up with options and cultural norms far different from those I faced at their age. Whether or not we support feminist issues, we have to agree that the women's movement has reshaped the attitudes and changed the choices for women today who are seeking ways to find meaning in life.

When my children were born in the early 1970s, the working mother received more criticism. During the 1980s, when my children were growing up, the pendulum began swinging in the opposite direction. Now a majority of women work outside the home. "Supermom" supposedly does it all and has it all, from a satisfying career to a clean kitchen and quality time with the kids. And now the stay-at-home mom feels more criticized for making a choice with less status, according to worldly standards.

Another historic trend affects this picture. Homemaking used to be a full-time job that guaranteed a woman a lifetime responsibility. Women had shorter life spans and spent more years in child raising. But as we began to live longer, have fewer children, and acquire more technology to take over the household chores, homemaking took less time.

Today, the stay-at-home mother's job is made up of two functions: homemaking, or cleaning and running the household, and caretaking, or rearing and caring for the children. Caring for children has great value for most women, but cleaning does not. So when the children start growing up and needing Mom less, she finds herself with more time for taking care of the house, which doesn't give her much satisfaction. If economics don't force her to think about choices, boredom often does.

My mother raised four children in an era when women were expected to stay at home, which she gladly did. When we left home, she faced a difficult transition, though eventually she prepared herself for a new career in real estate. I raised three children in a transitional era, working at home while they were growing up. But my daughters talk more about careers than I did, and they're preparing themselves for those careers better than I did. They intend to spend several years settling into those careers before they face the responsibility of having children.

As a mother, I hope they face their transitional choices later in life as middle ground-ers, maintaining the best of their traditional values from the past while looking forward to healthy changes in the future. I hope their economic situation enables them to have a choice about staying home with little children and their values affirm the importance of the choice; I hope my daughters see mothering as a valid "middle career" choice that will last as long as their children need them. I hope they embrace change as God's exciting path toward growth. These are my prayers from my mid-life perspective, but I know the choices will be theirs, and I will be an observer, not a director.

Willingness to change means an openness to embracing life's transitions, and as I've applied that to myself, I've found another ingredient in this willingness: the willingness, support, and understanding of the spouse. I've identified my generation as transitional, which means we face the greatest challenge in embracing change. We grew up in one set of norms, and now we're living in a different set.

This change has caused a problem for some marriages in my generation. A woman stayed home with her children while they were young, for instance, but as they grew up and needed her less, she desired new challenges. Sometimes her husband felt threatened by her restlessness or took it personally, and consciously or unconsciously, he discouraged rather than encouraged her desire for change and growth. As one husband confessed, he feels as though someone switched the rules on him. He married a woman who wanted to stay at home, and suddenly, staying home isn't enough for her. He doesn't understand, not because he doesn't want to but because he hasn't been through the same "consciousness raising" many women go through. Reaching an understanding takes communication, compromise, and sacrifice. Women who choose to avoid facing that struggle sometimes end up doting on their grown children instead of moving on to something else.

I'm thankful that throughout our parenting years, Lynn has encouraged me in new projects. He's never given a flat no, we've always talked about my choices, and he's shown his support by coming home early or arranging weekends to help me carve out quiet times to meet writing deadlines. When I'm pressed, he stops for take-out food on the way home. By the same token, I've tried not to make unreasonable demands that jeopardize his full-time responsibilities at his office. A marriage is a partnership. On our wedding day, we vowed to love and care for each other. Living out that commitment means being *willing* to change and encouraging the partner's growth through the seasons of life.

The Bible is filled with examples of people who turned their faces toward change rather than away. I think of Sarah, who willingly gave up the comforts and security of the known (her home and country) for the unknown (traveling around and heading for Canaan with Abraham). Though she surely faced hardships and fears, God rewarded her willingness to change with Isaac, a miracle baby.

I also think of Ruth, who willingly let go of her past and followed her mother-in-law, Naomi, from Moab, Ruth's homeland, back to Naomi's homeland in Israel. But God rewarded her willingness to change with her eventual marriage to Boaz.

Mary, the mother of Jesus, showed a trusting willingness to change when she, a young virgin engaged to be married, received a visit from the angel Gabriel, who told her she carried the Son of God in her womb. She must have faced a huge uncertainty about her future, yet within moments of getting the incredible news, she turned her face toward change and spoke those powerful words of willingness that have transcended the centuries: "I am the Lord's servant. . . . May it be to me as you have said" (Luke 1:38).

In addition to *willingness* to change, we must *prepare* for change. Just as the student's path through high school ends with graduation, so our path through the seasons of life takes us into the empty nest. We should not be surprised by the result. We experience nudging reminders all along the way, and we have time to prepare.

High-school students are prodded to prepare for changes more than parents facing the changes of mid-life. Students are constantly urged to think about choices, and graduation forces them to make choices. Parents looking toward the changes of the empty nest must devise their own steps of preparation.

I know several men and women who went back to school part-time and paced their classes so that graduation coincided with their youngests' graduation from high school. In their first few years without kids at home, they were absorbed with new jobs. Change did not catch them by surprise. They prepared for it.

Others seek the help of career counselors in clarifying their choices and making decisions as their children go off to grade school and junior high. Fathers, too, face more flexibility as their children leave home. One well-known Christian leader refused all out-of-town speaking invitations during his sons' high school years, but as the last one neared graduation, he and his wife prepared a plan that enabled him to travel and encourage renewal in churches across the country.

Parents may feel more freedom as their children grow up and leave, but they may have less flexibility, because their financial burdens increase as those children enter college. With two in college and a third on her way, we face the time of greatest financial need in our family. That need becomes part of our planning and preparation process in these years.

In *Pathfinders*, author Gail Sheehy identified *anticipation* as the first phase of a life passage, a time when we look toward a transition with an openness to its possibilities. It's a time of preparation, when we gather up the best parts of our past and discover the patterns and passions that point us toward the future. And then, with courage, we march toward graduation—or commencement, which means "beginning."

8

Graduation: Celebrating a Rite of Passage

One bright spring afternoon, Derek brought home the order blank for graduation announcements and plunked it down on the kitchen counter. "How many announcements should we order? Fifty?" he joked with a grin.

Obviously, visions of presents danced in his head.

I had a different vision: relatives and friends opening the announcement and seeing it as a plea for a present. After all, if we knew them well enough to send a graduation announcement, they knew us well enough to realize Derek was graduating *without* getting an official notice. And in most cases, the announcements would go to the same people we'd been hounding for years with every school fund-raising request, from cheese and sausage sales to pledges for walk-a-thons to car washes.

Suddenly, though, I had one bright thought. When those friends and relatives realized Derek's graduation would bring an end to some of those requests, surely they'd be delighted to join in the celebration! With that benevolent motivation, Derek and I got to work making a list. Counting a few extra for the scrapbook, we settled on twenty announcements, which was the smallest number we could order.

This little scenario served as a preview to the jumble of feelings and responsibilities surrounding the hectic ritual of a high-school graduation. Soon Derek began receiving party invitations and letters about school and church activities. The calendar filled up quickly, and we found ourselves swept up in a whirlwind of events that finally ground to a halt in a huge auditorium on a cool June morning, where an endless line of red-and-white caps and gowns marched down an aisle to the tune of "Pomp and Circumstance." Though I always planned to cry at that moment, I did not. I felt exhausted and numbly removed from the deeper meaning of this milestone in our family's life. I was an observer, watching an event I was part of in some remote way.

By the time Lindsay graduated a year later, we had a better perspective. We learned to enlarge the graduation celebration to enrich the meaning of this rite of passage. But that takes some careful planning, because family celebrations and moments for reflection can get lost in frenzied schedules.

Make a Celebration

In our contemporary culture, we don't *make* many celebrations, especially those that mark family transitions or passages. As Christians, celebration should be a regular part of our lives, especially the celebration of thanks for the good things God gives us, like marriage, family, reaching maturity, and marking transitions. Richard Foster, in *Celebration of Discipline,* wrote, "Celebration is at the heart of the way of Christ. He entered the world on a high note of jubilation: 'I bring you good news of a great joy,' cried the angel . . . (Luke 2:10). He left the world bequeathing his joy to the disciples: 'These things I have spoken to you that my joy may be in you and your joy may be full' (John 15:11). . . . Celebration brings joy into life, and joy makes us strong."[1]

The Bible describes many joyous festivities that went on for days, but our lives today lack the spirit of those joyous celebrations. So we need to seize the opportunities to *make* celebrations out of the significant events in our lives—like graduation.

The celebration of graduation does not have to be confined to the day of the commencement ceremony. Graduation is a season of weeks on either side of that event, and it offers plenty of time for family events and quiet moments apart from the hectic schedule of awards assemblies, parties, senior prom, senior picnic, and the baccalaureate.

Most of those planned events naturally focus on the students, and parents are observers. In one sense, the observer role seems fitting, since our parenting has reached a mostly observing stage by graduation. Yet, in another sense, we need to find personal ways to process and express our own responses to the meaning of this milestone. My moments of nostalgia descended upon me at odd times during those weeks before and after graduation, often when least expected, and those moments were nearly lost in the hectic round of activities, because they had no specific outlet or focal point of expression.

Graduation Ceremony

For students, the graduation ceremony serves as an appropriate focal point for the confusing emotions they've been experiencing in the weeks leading up to the event. They've been considering the upcoming changes in their lives, getting together with friends, reminiscing, crying and laughing, fearing and knowing things will never be quite the same again in their circle of friends or family structure. "What are you doing?" and "Where are you going?" are common questions they ask each other. Most know their immediate plans; a few don't. But one thing is certain: Life is about to change forever.

Then comes the traditional ceremony. For years, they've watched others participate in similar ceremonies, rich with symbols and rituals. They dress in special caps and gowns; they march to a familiar tune ("Pomp and Circumstance," which means "splendid ceremonious display"); student speakers remind them of their shared past; adult speakers challenge them to think about the future.

Appropriate songs and entertainment add to the sense of celebration, and it all ends with the students' being pronounced graduates as they move their tassels from one side of their caps to the other. Finally, they toss their hats high into the air, another symbol of celebration. Pictures are taken, tears are shed, and when it's all over, the new graduates know they have participated in a life-altering moment they'll never forget. Later, they turn in their caps and gowns but keep their tassels and hang them from their rearview mirrors or on bulletin boards in their bedrooms.

The traditional graduation ceremony attaches deep significance to the meaning of leaving high school and entering into a new challenge. It marks their rite of passage. It leaves them with tangible symbols. It creates a lasting memory. It contains all the ingredients of a ceremony and becomes the "period" at the end of their high-school sentence.

I thought about these ingredients and the importance of ceremony at Christmastime the year in between Derek's and Lindsay's graduations. I had heard about a celebration created by our local hospice organization. Hospices aid dying people and their families, and each Christmas, our local group hosts an observance for those people who have lost loved ones within the last year. Because Christmas is a time of great loneliness for people in grief, this ceremony gives them a focal point to express their feelings. Each family lights a candle and celebrates the loved one's life by showing pictures or telling the others of special memories. People who attend find great comfort in the ritual.

This celebration contains the traditional ingredients. A ceremony has a clear purpose: It seeks to name and honor what we value, and this ceremony honors the deceased and validates the grief of the survivors. It connects the past to the present and future. It offers an opportunity to reminisce, which helps people process their feelings of grief and loss. The candles and pictures become symbols, and when taken home and displayed, they are tangible reminders of the celebration and offer continuing comfort.

As I considered the hospice ceremony, I understood at once how the graduation ceremony clearly meets the needs of students by connecting the past to the present and future, giving them an opportunity to reminisce and creating symbols as tangible reminders of the ceremony. But I also began to understand why parents might feel like observers and emerge feeling a bit numb.

When I served on the graduation committee the year after Derek's graduation, we talked about this unmet need and decided to offer an evening for parents called "Graduation: Marking the Milestone from a Parent's Point of View." An especially sensitive high-school counselor and mother of two recent graduates led the evening. She offered helpful information about graduation and family transitions, and then she encouraged discussion from the parents, who were invited to bring any special mementos or reflections about growing up and graduation.

I brought two collages of photographs and told of an important moment of understanding that happened in the midst of Derek's graduation season. It might have been lost or forgotten except for this tangible symbol—the collage—that still comforts me today.

The moment came on a Saturday afternoon about a week before graduation. Already I'd begun to notice how this season softened my heart, making me aware of how quickly Derek had grown up—

while I had turned my back or blinked. That particular afternoon, as he reached for the car keys on his way out the door, I didn't see a young man about to graduate and go off to college nearly 1,500 miles away. I saw a little boy in a Batman cape and bathing suit with Band-Aids on both knees, speeding out the door so his cape would float instead of droop. I saw a mischievous little guy with dimples who liked to push the button on the garage door opener and then leap to catch the handle so he could ride the door to the top, even though he always landed in a crumpled heap on the ground below.

"See you later, Mom," he said that afternoon in a voice that must have grown deep overnight. And when the door closed, I felt suddenly sad about this little boy leaving home. So I went to the shelf above my desk and pulled down the plastic box stuffed with his pictures, report cards, and swim team ribbons I'd been saving since his Batman days.

For the rest of the afternoon, I sorted through that stuff, organizing everything into categories. I began lining up his school pictures, starting with preschool, challenging myself to find a picture for each year. It was like putting pieces of a puzzle together. At last I had a complete set, which I pasted in two rows on a piece of poster board. A LITTLE BOY GROWS UP, I penned across the top in large letters. Then I thumbtacked the collage to the wall in the front hall.

As I stood back to look at it, I saw a dependent, dimple-faced little boy slowly growing into a confident, independent young man—and the truth hit me. The person I felt sad about leaving—the one I longed to cuddle and hold close and protect—was not the one graduating. It was the dimple-faced little boy who needed me to put Band-Aids on his knees and pick him up when he fell down. But the "finished product" in the senior picture at other end of the lineup had a look of confident readiness. I didn't want to hold on to that person. I wanted to celebrate his achievement of maturity and be his cheerleader as he entered a new chapter of his life. Though his confidence and eagerness would surely be tested and sometimes shaken in the years to come, I wanted to shout, "Yes! You can do it! You're ready!"

That realization freed me from some of my sadness. In bringing order to that box of pictures, I also brought a sense of order to my confusion about holding on and letting go. I want to hold on to a child who needs me, but I want to let go of a child who is ready to go. Only then will his love be able to grow from an immature love that says, "I love you because I need you," to a mature love that says, "I need you because I love you."

I want to share a mature love with my grown children.

I made the same kind of collage with Lindsay's class pictures, and her lineup told a similar story of a grinning little girl growing through a self-conscious stage and blossoming into a confident young woman.

Her pictures reminded me that kids are like batches of cookies. God gives us the privilege of being their "bakers," so we put them into the oven of our control and protection. If we take them out too soon, they'll be mushy and soft. But if we leave them in the oven too long, they'll be burned. We have to take them out of the oven at just the right time. Lindsay's senior picture said, "This is the right time. I'll still make mistakes and I'll still fail, but I'm ready to try."

I told my stories and showed my collages to the other parents that night. Those collages, now laminated, have become tangible symbols that remind me of those truths about holding on and letting go, and I keep them in a place where I can see them and feel comforted by what I learned.

Other parents told their stories, too, and we ended the evening with some quiet moments of reflection followed by a tape of the song "Wind Beneath My Wings." As I left, I considered the potential of such a ceremony for parents through our schools or churches, a celebration with an inspirational speaker and appropriate opportunities to talk and reflect on our feelings as our seniors graduate.

In addition to the emotional side of graduation, there are some practical considerations. As we faced the experience two years in a row, we talked with other families and formulated some tips about the celebration that helped our second year go smoother than the first. Here are some practical suggestions:

1. Communicate to compare expectations. Kids often think of graduation in terms of celebrating with friends, while parents are apt to visualize leisurely family gatherings with Grandma and Grandpa. Several weeks before graduation, we began marking obligations on the calendar, and where we found conflicts, we discussed our expectations and compromised. The day of graduation often presents the greatest potential for conflict, because out-of-town guests and relatives want to see the graduate, who often has his or her own agenda. For this reason, our school plans a Saturday late-morning graduation, which gives people time to arrive and then time afterward for families to celebrate together before the students go out with their friends. Since graduation is known for wild parties and drinking, comparing expectations also includes discussions about freedom and social responsibilities.

2. Plan family activities. A family needs time to honor and celebrate this milestone of change and achievement together. But graduation is a season, not simply a single event, so special family activities can be planned at times separate from the graduation ceremony. We planned family vacations around driving both Derek and Lindsay to college at the end of the summer, which fulfilled that ceremonial ingredient of connecting the past to the future. Closer to graduation, we planned a party for families of kids who went to school together since kindergarten. We invited some teachers and spent an evening reliving memories.

3. Celebrate the past. Reminiscing is an essential ingredient of graduation, because remembering the blessings of the past brings comfort and hope for the future. The Old Testament is filled with examples of people using feasts and memorials to celebrate God's past faithfulness. When the Israelites passed over the Jordan River, the Lord instructed them to build a memorial of stones to remind them of how He delivered them through difficulties. Family photos and videos become great "rocks" for this kind of reminiscing. We pulled out our family photo albums and placed them on a coffee table so everyone visiting around graduation could leaf through them. We watched hilarious (and sometimes embarrassing) home videos. We remembered camping trips, Christmases, and 4-H horse shows. Our family memories became our rock-solid reminders that God, who so richly blessed us in the past, would surely bless us in the future.

4. Celebrate the future. For both parents and adolescents, looking toward the future with anticipation is as important as reminiscing about the past with gratitude. We hung up sweatshirts with their college logos as tangible reminders of their future plans, and we talked often about their hopes for the next year of their lives. While celebrating the past is based on *facts,* celebrating the future is based on *faith* in God's promises.

One day when I found myself dwelling on the past more than anticipating the future, I drew a personal time line, starting with our marriage. I added some obvious milestones, including the birth of each child, memorable trips, and job accomplishments, and ended with the graduation date. I then began filling in the rest of the blank line with hopes for the rest of my life. Soon, I found the "future" part of my line crowded with aims like visiting the Holy Land, riding a bike over a mountain, writing a great love story, planning a wedding (at least one child will surely get married), being a grandmother . . . my list went on. I celebrated the future by fastening my eyes on this tangible symbol of all I looked forward to.

5. Give them a blessing. In biblical times, fathers traditionally sent their children off with a blessing, sometimes to signify their inheritance, but also to symbolize their independence. They had been released from parental control and placed in God's greater hands for protection and guidance. One graduate received a box containing his mother's apron strings, symbolizing her recognition of her son's emancipation. When Lindsay graduated, we gave her a ring with three small stones. "As you go far from home," we told her, "wear this ring and remember that you are like the middle stone of this setting, surrounded on both sides by our love."

Some give the gift of a new Bible with meaningful, personal inscriptions. Others write personal keepsake letters to their graduates. Some say they wish they could write such letters but don't have a "way with words." If that's your situation, you can borrow words by giving a copy of someone else's letter that conveys the appropriate message. Here's an anonymous letter entitled "A Letter to My Graduate":

> I cannot buy you a set of morals; I cannot build you a sense of responsibility; I cannot manufacture for you a concern and compassion; I cannot make yours a compelling, faithful, loyal spirit; I cannot give you the ability to love.
>
> I have no fortune to will you which will gain you popularity, make you a philanthropist, or help you leave memorials for charity.
>
> I own no secret formula for success nor any new philosophy. I've never written a book of wisdom.
>
> I cannot send you away into the world on your own, with only beautiful pictures in your memory, for you have seen me cry faithless tears of despair; you have seen me shake my fist in anger; you have witnessed ugliness in my time of weakness.
>
> But these things I cannot give you are all yours in Christ Jesus.
>
> As you accept your diploma, severing your relations with your school, you step into new relationships with parents, friends, and the world. The "apron strings" that have been lengthened as you matured must soon be cut. You have earned more than freedom. You have proved

yourself trustworthy, dependable, and mature enough to try your wings, but I will be "on call" throughout my life.

You are fully accountable to God, your Heavenly Father, who loves you far more than I, who has riches in store beyond your comprehension, but who expects much, sees, and knows—also beyond your comprehension.

I commit you to His care as the fire of the world tests the gold of your character. And I will always be in prayer for you.

Love from Your Parent

Giving a book is another great way to borrow a message. One of my favorites is *As You Leave Home,* a personal letter from Jerry Jenkins to his son Dallas, who was graduating from high school. Jenkins offered advice about life and put the feelings of parental love into words, describing the emotions that catch us by surprise as our children leave home. Here's a sample:

Only my selfishness would tell me I'd rather have you stay than go. That's the same selfishness that is jealous of heaven when a beloved saint is taken. That covetousness would cup a butterfly in our palms and withhold it from its purpose, its freedom.

So as you think about me with whatever emotion is appropriate, feel free not to focus on my pain, my longing—yes, my grief. It's a hurdle. It's my burden, not yours. I inform you of it for a higher purpose: to let you know the depth of my love for you.[2]

Books of advice are popular gifts for seniors, probably because graduation is one of those few times in life when adults have the right to pass pithy truths down to the next generation. We also consider them good investments, because we picture our offspring hungrily poring over them when they're far away and need some reminders from home. Popular books of this era include a collection of devotionals: *What About God Now That You're Off to College,* by Helen R. Neinast and Thomas Ettinger; *The On My Own Handbook: 100 Secrets of Success to Prepare Young People for Life in the Real World,* by Bobb Biehl; *All I Really Need to Know I Learned in Kindergarten,* by Robert Fulghum, who gives such advice as "Share everything; play fair; and say you're sorry when you hurt somebody"; and *Life's Little Instruction Book,* volumes 1 and 2, collections of one-liners written by H. Jackson Brown, Jr., to his graduating senior.

"I read years ago that it was not the responsibility of parents to pave the road for their children, but to provide a road map," Brown wrote. "That's how I hoped he would use these mind and heart reflections." Random entries include the following: "Remember other people's birthdays; Give yourself a year and read the Bible cover to cover; Strive for excellence, not perfection; Pray not for things, but for wisdom and courage; Call your mother."[3]

Of course I underlined the last one in red before giving the book to our two leaving home. I also added a few one-liners borrowed from Max Lucado: "When no one is watching, live as if someone is; Only harbor a grudge when God does; Pray twice as much as you fret; Succeed at home first; When you can't trace God's hand, trust his heart."[4]

Gift giving is a traditional part of the graduation celebration, and I kept a list of appropriate and appreciated gifts, those we gave or received or wished we'd given. Here are some suggestions:

*Books—a good Bible, an advice book, a book of daily devotionals, or a resource book such as a dictionary, atlas, thesaurus, or Bible commentary

*Family photograph album—filled with photos of family and friends

*Address book—with family addresses, plus another page listing family birthdays

🎀Write-home kit—including notecards, postcards, stamps, and pens

🎀Personalized stationery

🎀Framed photograph of family—engraved with "There's No Place Like Home"

🎀Framed collage for pictures of friends

🎀Poster picture from familiar area around home

🎀Wall calendar with pictures from home—again marked with special dates

🎀Backpack or book bag

🎀 Luggage or duffel bag

🎀Sleeping bag

🎀Solar-powered calculator

🎀Day-Timer/date book

🎀Alarm clock or clock radio

🎀Sewing kit; tool kit; first aid kit

🎀Desk kit, including scissors, tape, correction fluid, paper clips, rubber bands

🎀Desktop mug (from hometown) filled with pens and pencils

🎀Flashlight

🎀Umbrella

🎀Plastic carry tote for bathroom supplies

🎀Iron; hot pot; popcorn popper

🎀Camera

🎀Telephone answering machine

🎀Monogrammed towels

🎀Makeup mirror

🎀Sweatshirt with logos from home

A graduation gift is meant to honor the person, celebrate past achievements, and offer encouragement for the future. The possibilities are endless, and rather than produce drudgery, the thought of giving graduation gifts can stretch the imagination and creativity. I know one couple who gave a former baby-sitter "dinner with a date." They picked up the graduate and her date and whisked them off to the top of a mountain near Boulder on a summer evening. There the young people found a picnic table set with tablecloth, china, and silver. They were served a gourmet meal by their older friends, who then disappeared on a short hike while the young couple enjoyed their meal.

In our family, we're now in a comforting lull between graduations; two down and one to go. But we know from experience that graduation is a milestone shared by a family, and we aim to make a celebration and a memory that becomes one of our rock-solid reminders of God's goodness in the history of our family.

Graduation is also one of God's gentle nudges that reminds us, "Change is coming. Get ready."

9

The Summer
Between

"*I*'m going down to the ditch, Mom," 18-year-old Derek told me as he came into the kitchen on a quiet summer afternoon.

"The ditch?" I questioned, surprised. I looked up from the mail I'd been reading.

"Yeah. I haven't been there for a long time, and I just feel like going. Anything wrong with that?"

"Nothing," I assured him as he walked out the door, wearing an old baseball cap and carrying his slingshot—both remnants of his childhood. Going down the hill through the fields to the irrigation ditch used to be the most normal thing for a little boy to do. Derek spent hours down there, climbing the huge cottonwood trees, swinging over the water on a rope, shooting his slingshot at old tin cans, or just exploring in his own make-believe forest. The ditch seemed a perfect place for a kid to go untie the knots in his life.

In time, his trips down to the ditch grew less frequent. Soccer and homework and friends seemed more important. Next came the keys to the car and driving back and forth to town, where the real action was. He hadn't been down to the ditch in years.

With high school behind him and college in front of him, Derek's priorities seemed to shift a bit. "This feels like an in-between summer," he told me. "I don't belong in high school anymore, but I don't yet belong in college, so I don't know where I belong." His two younger sisters accused him of acting moody and weird. I told them he was trying to "hold on and let go."

This Saturday, he'd been downstairs in his room, sorting his stuff into three piles: one to give away, one to store, and one to pack up for college. Maybe he couldn't decide which pile the hat and slingshot belonged in. Maybe he thought a trip down to the ditch would help him figure it out.

The phone rang, and from somewhere in the house, I heard 17-year-old Lindsay calling Derek.

"He's gone down to the ditch," I told her.

A long silence followed. Then Lindsay suddenly appeared at my elbow in the kitchen. "He's *what?*" she said. She rolled her eyes when I repeated myself. "Now I'm *really* worried about him," she muttered, leaving the room. And then, like the town gossip bursting with shocking news, she yelled loudly downstairs to her younger sister, who was playing the piano. "Kendall, did you hear that? Derek's *gone down to the ditch!*" She might as well have said he was playing in the sandbox.

The music stopped abruptly. "You're not serious!" 13-year-old Kendall replied, sounding equally incredulous.

"Hey, you two, back off," I told them, feeling protective of Derek's feelings. "Give him some space, and *please* don't tease him when he comes back." But even as I said the words, I knew that was an impossibility.

About an hour later, Derek returned.

"How's everything down at the ditch?" I heard one of his sisters ask him. But he went right to his room without answering.

Later I found the hat and slingshot in the "to store" pile.

That summer seemed like an "in-between summer" for the whole family, because we all teetered on the brink of a major change that would alter the structure of our family forever. Since we'd never walked this path before, none of us knew how to handle our anticipation. Lindsay and Kendall opted for teasing, as siblings are apt to do, while I opted for melodramatic melancholy, as moms seem prone to do.

Most of the time, I tried to control my display of sadness, because I didn't want to burden Derek with my feelings as I thought about his leaving home. Yet sometimes, as I watched him eating cereal or reading the newspaper, I spontaneously hugged him.

"Sometimes I need to do that," I explained with a quiver in my voice.

I think he understood.

I rationalized on the basis of a Sunday-morning memory from many years ago, when he was nine and lying in a crumpled heap on an examining table in the doctor's office.

"We have juvenile diabetes here," the doctor announced quietly after completing a couple of tests. The room swirled around me, and my tears came quickly, but I turned my face and tried to hide them from Derek.

"It's okay for him to see your sadness," the doctor told me later. "He needs to know you love him and that what happens to him matters to you."

Sometimes I hugged him that summer because the thought of his leaving home *mattered*. And I wanted him to know it.

Other moms get melodramatic and melancholy during the in-between summer. I ran into a friend who was facing the same challenge, with her oldest leaving home in the fall. "Something terrible is happening," she admitted. "He can do no wrong in my eyes.

Every time I look at him, I feel weepy and get all huggy. I dote on him something fierce."

"You do have two other children," I teasingly reminded her.

"Oh, yes," she replied vaguely. "And what are their names?"

During that summer, I also began clinging to those everyday family experiences I used to take for granted, like riding in a car or going out to eat. "Let's all go *together*," I begged as we tried to figure out cars and transportation to and from church. "It may be our *last time*."

When my mother was dying of emphysema years ago, we had an unspoken pact: Let's turn regular events into family celebrations, because this *might be our last*. We gathered often to celebrate birthdays and Easter and the Fourth of July—for more than two years. The number of last-time gatherings almost became a family joke, but I'm still thankful for the effort and all those memories.

Maybe all mothers instinctively respond like Mary, the mother of Jesus, who purposefully gathered experiences and conversations and stored them like treasures in her heart to ponder later. Surely, her heart full of treasures became a source of comfort as she had to "let go" of the Jesus she knew and raised as a child.

During the in-between summer, I took lots of family pictures and even began saving those silly little notes we left each other on the kitchen counter. For years, I worried that our family was becoming a disconnected group of people who communicated mostly through notes. But I started gathering up those scraps of paper, knowing that someday they might give me a comforting reminder of this era of our lives.

Here's a sample:

"Mom, sorry I was a pest this morning. Thanks for your help."

"Mom and Dad, I went to Corey's and then Bill's and then I'm not sure."

"Derek, Corey called, Jasmine didn't, and the garbage is still calling you."

"Mom and Dad, I'm at Susan's. Love Derek. [Note added by little sister: "Yea! He finally went out with a girl!"]

"Everyone in this family owes the youngest member some money. Mom-$2; Lindsay-$5; Dad-$6 for ice cream on Mother's Day. Pay up."

"Mom and Dad, look what came in the mail [a training schedule for college basketball]. I'm at the gym working out."

"Derek, I need your help today in (1) Remembering Mom's birthday; (2) Cleaning the patio. Dad"

"I went out with Corey and Bill . . . just like old times . . . probably for the last time."

During that same summer, Lindsay went away for a month to work at a Young Life camp, giving me a preview of an extended separation. Though our kids had been gone from home for a week or two in the past, this was the longest stretch of separation I had faced, and I had a hard time getting used to not knowing what she was doing each day or how she was feeling; I missed being part of the daily context of her life. As time passed, my eyes grew hungry for the sight of her. By the time she arrived home, I knew I still faced some tough weaning, but the experience also reminded me that going away to camp or leaving home for brief periods of time is good experience—for the kids and for us.

The summer wasn't a total love-in of hugs and kisses. We still faced our battles, mostly over control issues. The main one centered on finding and keeping a summer job. We had different opinions about the appropriate time frame for finding one and the definition of a decent one. When Derek slept in instead of getting up early to check the classified ads, or when he took a job and then quit a few days later to look for a better one, it rankled Lynn and me a bit. "That's not the way to do it," we said, and then we realized that what we meant was, "That's not our way of doing it." Though it might be appropriate for parents to tell a five-year-old when to get up and what to do, it is inappropriate to tell an almost-19-year-old. We remembered the guidelines used with parent-adolescent control issues:

•Maintaining the relationship is more important than being right or being powerful.

•A control issue is really a battle over "Who's in control here?" and we don't need to win that battle. We can give away some control and keep some.

•We're not going to tell him what to do (or force him to do something); we'll tell him what *we'll* do. We'll seek change where we have the power to change—with ourselves.

•We'll give him choices. He makes choices (which gives him control) and accepts the consequences of his choices (which is how the real world works).

In the summer job battle, Lynn and I knew Derek was more important than his summer job, and having a relationship with him was more important than proving ourselves right or in control. So we defined the most important issue; it wasn't how or when he got a summer job, but that he earn a certain amount of money over the summer to put toward his first year of college, an amount we'd agreed upon months earlier.

Our control was in the statement of what we were willing to do. We'd pay for room and board, tuition, and books the first year; he needed to earn his spending money. If he made less money, he had less money to spend. So we didn't need to nag him about getting a summer job. The choice and consequences were his. He had control over his part of the situation.

Handling control issues with teenagers means pulling back, identifying the areas of control, and then keeping some and giving some away. But pulling back—or deparenting—is sometimes the hardest part of parenting to learn.

Looking Ahead—Issues to Settle

During the in-between summer, college-bound students face many issues that are new to them: choosing or contacting roommates, handling finances, and understanding parental expectations while away at school. The summer will pass quickly, and the last hectic days before a student leaves are not good times for meaningful discussions. The weeks in the middle of the summer offer a better opportunity to settle issues that might cause conflict or misunderstanding if left to the last minute.

Roommates. If the student is going away from home, the roommate issue is a major concern. The school usually sends a housing application that allows the student to request a certain dorm and make a roommate request, or to give specific information that helps the school match up roommates. Many colleges—especially smaller ones—pride themselves on doing a good job of connecting strangers who have lots in common and quickly become good friends.

Both our incoming freshmen did some homework over the summer and found that dormitories have personalities that seem to endure through the years. One is for studious students; another has a reputation for being extra social. Both Derek and Lindsay were headed for schools with coed dorms, men living on one floor and women on another. (Some schools have men and women living on the same floor and sharing the same bathrooms, which would be difficult—nay, *impossible*—for this mom to take.)

To match up roommates, housing forms ask, Are you a morning or night person? Early or late riser? Introvert or extrovert? Messy or neat? Quiet and studious? Interested in school activities, athletics, or outreach ministries? They also ask about music preferences, hobbies and interests, academic interests, and "anything else you want us to know about you as we make your roommate assignment."

"Should I mark 'messy'?" one of ours asked in filling out the forms.

"No!" I answered emphatically. "Even though I've been telling you that for the past 15 years, college gives you an opportunity to turn over a new leaf!"

After completing the forms and sending them back, the student waits . . . and waits . . . with great anticipation for the name of the person he or she will live with for the next year. After that name is received, there's another jittery period: "Who calls whom first, or should I write a letter and send a picture?" For kids who have spent their lives making friends in person, this kind of communication seems a risky new experience.

"What do I say to him?" Derek questioned, agonizing over the letter he kept trying to write. "If I say too much about myself, he'll think I'm stuck on myself."

A year later, when Lindsay went through the same process, she called her new roommate right away. "She sounds great," Lindsay said after hanging up.

Some of her friends didn't have that same good feeling after the first communication. One nearly cried after her new roommate phoned.

"I'm an intelligent blonde, but I have a couple habits you might not like," she said. "I sing to myself a lot. When I'm in a good mood, I dance to the music I hear in my head. My appearance is different. I shaved part of my hair off several years ago, and I like to wear things that surprise and catch the attention of others." Then, before saying good-bye, she suggested they do their dorm room in a jungle theme.

"I don't think we'll have much in common," this friend said after hanging up.

Finances. Even before a student makes a final choice of schools, parents need to clarify what part of the bill they're paying. The expenses break down into several categories: *academic*, including tuition, room and board, books, and supplies; *clothing; recreational*, including fun money for movies and pizza and sports events; *incidentals*, including laundry, toiletries, haircuts, and phone bills. This list is not inclusive, but the idea is to take time to discuss specific areas and clarify where the money will come from, the amounts, and the responsibility for keeping track of it. Learning how to budget—stretching out a certain amount of money to last a whole semester—is one of the freshman's greatest lessons, according to our two college students. Learning to be frugal is another. When students start paying for their own shampoo and hair conditioner, they're amazed how much longer a bottle lasts.

The attempt to be frugal can lead to misunderstandings. If the parents and student agree that the student will pay for all toiletries, but then the student quietly wipes out the family supply of toothpaste, deodorant, and shampoo before leaving for college, the parents might get upset. Settle the issue of when the paying starts—before it becomes a problem.

The whole challenge of learning to budget can be learned in steps through high school, especially when a student gets a part-time or summer job and begins earning money. The questions about who pays for what and where that money goes are the beginning of budgeting.

Phone bills are a separate issue. Most college dorms provide phones or at least have phone jacks in the rooms. Then the choice is whether to buy or rent a phone and which long-distance company to use. Competition among long-distance carriers means more options for consumers these days, and comparison shopping lets you see which plan best meets your needs.

We purchased a system that allows our students to call us anytime on an 800 number, and those calls go on our bill. If a student goes to an out-of-state college, long-distance phone bills become a factor in the budget. They're important, especially the first year away from home, but often forgotten when considering the expense of going away to school. We also covered phone calls to their siblings. (We consider that a wise investment in family relationships, because they look forward to talking to each other rather than trying to decide if calling is worth the money.) And we told them they could call their Christian mentors, older people who had been important to them in our community, especially during that first year when they needed encouragement.

Transportation and cars require money and upkeep. Our two took bicycles to school, so transportation home at Christmas became the major chunk of this part of the budget.

Health insurance and insurance against theft or loss of property are related issues, and though some schools offer inexpensive insurance plans, most college students remain covered by their parents' health insurance and homeowner's policies while in school.

Parents' expectations. In the rush to get organized and pack up, it's easy to overlook discussions about parents' expectations regarding grades, priorities, and communication home. Lynn and I tried to clarify and agree upon these issues between the two of us, and then we planned several opportunities to spend time with our freshman-to-be over the summer, usually lunch or dinner out, just the three of us. Again, every family will have different expectations, but the important thing is to clarify and clearly communicate them. Though going on to college is taken for granted by many students, it is still a privilege and responsibility, and what a student gets out of the experience is largely based on the student's attitude about priorities.

Grades are not our primary concern; learning is. But grades are a valid reflection of how the student is doing. We didn't set a minimum grade point average. College students are apt to drop almost a whole letter grade from high school, and our kids agreed to aim for mostly *B*'s. Grades are more important if they plan to go on to graduate school. But our priorities included learning to think critically and express themselves in a clear and organized way, both in writing and verbally; to work diligently and have a balanced college experience, combining academics, spiritual growth, and an investment in relationships and activities. We encouraged them to interact with professors and get into study groups.

In preparation for those academic expectations, we discussed study skills and time management, which college students claim is their most difficult challenge during the freshman year. College life is known for its distractions and new freedoms, and lack of self-discipline or the inability to say no causes problems. "Set up some systems ahead of time," the colleges advised. So we discussed whether they're morning or night people, when they experience their best hours of concentration, and how they might commit to using those hours. Will they study in the dorms or the library? Will they sign up for the freshman study skills workshop? They carried some tools with them such as calendars and assignment sheets, systems that worked well in high school.

To-do lists. A myriad of other obligations popped up, including dentists' appointments. (*"Everyone* gets their wisdom teeth out before college," Lindsay told us, sounding frightened. Not everyone does, but Lindsay did on the dentist's advice.) Additional important to-do's are physical checkups, eye exams, prescription updates, and the task of shopping for clothes. What we began to learn and they began to believe is that clothes don't matter as much in college as they did in high school. So except for some basics, we held off until they got to campus and saw what they needed.

Packing Up

"I might as well pack everything. Then I won't forget anything or end up without something I need," our college freshman said. That's a temptation—until you think about the size of the room and the fact that another person (maybe two) will be doing the same thing. "Think small; think less; think organized" was the advice we got. Check with the roommate so stereos, little refrigerators, and any other large items aren't duplicated. Otherwise, packing up means deciding what one can live with and live without. Many college catalogues offer detailed lists, but here are some of the basics:

- Clothes
- Sports equipment
- Books, desk supplies
- Bed linens (including mattress pad, sheets, and a comforter instead of blankets)
- Towels
- Luggage, backpack
- Sleeping bag
- Room decorations (pillows, desk lamp, bulletin board,

pictures)

*Iron (with automatic shutoff)
*Alarm clock
*Hair dryer, curling iron
*Bathroom carryall, toiletries
*Sewing kit (including safety pins)
*First aid kit
*Stationery kit (including stamps)
*Wastebasket, hamper
*Extension cords and heavy tape (always needed on moving-in day)
*Closet organizers such as multiple skirt or pant hangers, folding shoe rack, plastic crates
*Extras, like camera, popcorn popper, hot pot, stereo

Ready, Set, Go!

For that in-between summer before Derek went to college, I put off thinking about driving him to school and saying good-bye. But as soon as I turned the calendar over to August, the reality set in. Instead of nebulous weeks and months away, our departure now could be counted in days.

"All summer, I've buried a place of sadness deep inside me where a little part of me hurts," I wrote in my journal. "I notice it when I see a reminder of fall, like back-to-school sales. I used to think of fall as a cozy family time of turning inward together. Now when I think of fall, I feel sad.

"Yet I also feel a nudge to move on, so I'm trying to fix up Derek's room. We've talked of getting rid of the water bed and painting the room. I'm frantic to do that before he goes so he knows we're doing it for him and the room feels familiar when he comes home. But his response surprised me."

"You're painting it *white?*" he asked, because it had been a deep blue.

"We need to lighten it up, don't you think?" I ventured.

"I guess I don't care. I won't be here anyway."

I felt sad at his indifference, but I shared some of his ambivalence. One part of me wanted to leave everything as it was, but another wanted to brighten it up, call the Salvation Army to haul away the old bed, and get a new bed in there so we finally had a decent place to offer an overnight guest while Derek was away. Before, we'd had only a sleeper sofa in the family room.

Part of me wanted to hold on; part of me wanted to move on.

Then there was the anticipation of the good-bye. I'd heard other mothers say they remembered that final good-bye as clearly as the moment of the child's birth. I began dreading the thought of saying good-bye and walking away from him.

When my mother was dying, I felt scared about saying good-bye to her. What would that last moment be like? How could I help her? Would I be strong for her? I worried about it for two years, and when that time finally came, God held both of our hands in a powerfully gentle way.

I hoped He would do the same when it came time to say good-bye to a child leaving home.

10

Saying Good-bye

As we pulled slowly out of the driveway in our old blue Suburban on that late August morning, Lindsay turned and poked Derek.

"Better take a good look, Bro," she teased, "because you won't see the old homestead again for a looong time."

"Like you'd really understand how that feels," he retorted sharply through clenched teeth as he pushed aside some suitcases and peered longingly out the back window until we rounded a corner and the house disappeared. He then turned with a sigh and rested his head on the back of the seat.

The car, jam-packed from floor to ceiling, held most of Derek's belongings as we began the journey that would forever change his life—and the life of our family. We were taking him off to college, halfway across the country in Tacoma, Washington. Though we billed the trip as a family vacation, we all dreaded the thought of saying good-bye and coming home without him. Yet each of us handled his or her feelings differently.

Lindsay teased. Kendall spoke more honestly. "This makes me sad," she said quietly, putting her hand on Derek's shoulder.

Lynn, the father and driver, concentrated on the road but kept glancing in the rearview mirror, trying to catch a glimpse of Derek as we pulled out on the highway.

I sat scrunched on a small section of the far-back seat with a bucket beside me. I hadn't slept at all the night before, and I felt sick.

I probably dreaded the good-bye most of all. That milestone moment comes to every parent and almost-grown child at different times under different circumstances and in different settings. It may be when an adolescent leaves for military service or a job away from home. It may be at an airport, at the end of an aisle in a church wedding, or in a driveway beside a car packed with personal belongings. It may be only the first of many major good-byes, but that first one feels like a gigantic turning point, especially to a mother. That's why I was determined to make the most of our last few days together.

From the moment we decided to turn the journey into a family vacation, I began to build expectations about our cozy closeness. I pictured us rolling up the windows, turning off the radio, and telling Derek everything he needed to know about life that we might have left out in the last 19 years. Undoubtedly, some of the good stuff would rub off on Lindsay and Kendall, too. I even began collecting appropriate tapes for the occasion from James Dobson, Tony Campolo, and Josh McDowell. I also brought a special journal to record significant conversations or thoughts. On the outside I wrote, "Journey Toward Good-bye."

Within the first few hours of the trip, however, I realized we might have different agendas, as each child disappeared into a private oblivion under the influence of a Walkman, listening to tapes by groups whose names didn't make sense to me.

Lessons Learned

So much for my preconceived plans, I decided. And in my journal, I noted *Lesson #1: Don't build unrealistic, inflexible expectations. Go with the flow.* Over the next four days, going with the flow brought some spontaneously great times. We tried all the house specialties in local restaurants along the way; we stopped and jogged around picturesque parks in small towns; we pulled over to read historical roadside markers; we explored other college campuses en route (just for comparison); and early one morning, we prayed together, praising God for His idea of families and asking His hand of protection and guidance on Derek's exciting year of opportunities. We even listened to one tape together.

I noted *Lesson #2: Enjoy life's irretrievable moments.*

We arrived in Tacoma early one afternoon, checked into a motel, and then took a look around the town, helping Derek get his bearings. We found the closest supermarket, drugstore, and medical facilities (because his small school offered only limited hours for campus health care). We also located the most convenient automatic teller machines for banking. Because Derek had a checking account and debit card from our bank at home, we did not open an account for him at a local bank. The debit card enabled him to obtain cash from automatic teller machines; it also worked in place of checks at many businesses. And most places accepted checks from an out-of-state bank as long as he had his driver's license for identification.

We had dinner together at a nice restaurant that night. I vowed not to dwell on my feelings of nostalgia, but the words *Last Supper* kept running through my mind.

Early the next morning, we arrived on campus to begin the process of moving Derek into room 333 in Todd Hall. I soon learned that moving in is a fascinating ritual for families and worthy of full-time observing. But since we had work to do, I had to settle for catching only the edges of the dynamics going on around us.

Shortly after 8:00 A.M., station wagons, RV's, U-Hauls, and minivans began pulling into the parking lots near the dormitories. Doors opened, and people spilled out, sometimes whole families, sometimes dads and sons or mothers and daughters. Except for exuberant younger siblings and a few outgoing fathers, everyone seemed a bit subdued, especially the freshmen. The outgoing fathers overcompensated for the tension, introducing themselves and their families to total strangers in the parking lots, while their embarrassed sons or daughters cowered in the background.

I noted *Lesson #3: Once on campus, be sensitive to your son's or daughter's feelings.*

Inside Derek's dorm, we found a check-in table, and from the periodic shrieks, we knew roommates were finding and greeting each other for the first time. Soon Derek found Erik from Salem, the other resident of room 333. They shook hands shyly, and then I hugged Erik enthusiastically. Suddenly I felt choked with emotion. "I've been praying for you every day since we got your name in the mail," I stammered, starting to cry. I didn't intend to get so sentimental, so I started worrying about myself. Undoubtedly, I'd be totally out of control by the end of the day.

I took a deep breath and shook hands with Erik's parents like a normal person. Then we all went down the long hall to find their new home.

"Nice," I heard myself say as I viewed the room, which was smaller than Derek's bedroom at home. It had one small window, two desks, two shelves, two closets, and two bunk beds. *Certainly sparse . . . certainly adequate,* I corrected myself. Then I realized they were right next door to the bathroom. *They'll never get any sleep,* I worried.

"Great!" Derek exclaimed. "We're right next door to the bathroom."

For the next couple of hours, we moved almost everything Derek owned into the small room, while Erik did the same. *Only a miracle will help them find a place for everything,* I thought, surveying the piles.

We left our moving duties mid-morning for the parent-orientation sessions. Traditionally, those meetings are held on every campus that first day to give parents information and help them through the time of saying good-bye to their students. Different schools have different theories about the length of these sessions, because once students arrive on campus, they're torn between the need (or obligation) to spend time with parents and the desire to get on with their lives and meet new people. When parents hang around too long, everyone begins to feel awkward.

Some campuses offer orientation sessions in the summer so parents don't have to linger long after they drive their kids to school. Some families send their sons or daughters to school alone, claiming they would rather visit a month or two after school starts, when the student is settled in and less distracted. Thus, many colleges schedule parents' weekends in October.

We wanted to gather as much firsthand information as we could about Derek's new home, so we filed into an auditorium with hundreds of other parents to hear the president talk about the freshman experience, "one of life's most significant transitions." He repeated the school's philosophy and goals, and he assured parents the school wanted to help students but would not replace the parents: "One mother called to complain that her son was having a hard time getting to class each morning, and she wondered if we could make sure he got out of bed. We care a great deal about our students' success in academics, but we want our college students to accept responsibility for their own choices and actions."

Roommates pose frequent challenges, he acknowledged, since most students are used to the privacy of their own rooms at home. "But just remember, learning to live with a college roommate is jolly good preparation for marriage!" I liked that thought so well that I noted *Lesson #4: Take advantage of orientation activities.*

Following the president's welcome, we met with Derek's academic adviser, toured the campus, and gathered for a picnic lunch on the quadrangle lawn. It was a perfect fall day, with a hint of red and orange in the trees and a new season in the air.

After lunch, we went back to the dorm for the last bit of unpacking. As we paraded down the hall, I overheard bits of family conversations coming from other rooms:

"Don't put your underwear in that drawer down there," one mother lectured her son. "You'll never reach it."

"You won't want your lamp there," another warned. "You'll never get enough light on your books."

"Your beds won't work like that," a father advised.

I had gotten pretty good at this "letting go" stuff, I smugly decided. I wasn't going to give Derek advice he didn't want. He needed to know we had confidence in his ability to make his own decisions. Besides, if he put his underwear in a drawer he couldn't reach, he'd figure it out. That was not my problem.

I wrote *Lesson #5: Let them be in charge of decisions about their rooms.*

My smugness didn't last long. Soon everything was unpacked, and I knew we were nearing the moment I'd been dreading. I assumed we'd say good-bye at the car. We'd grope around for some meaningful words, hug, and then the four of us would climb in and drive away, leaving Derek standing alone and waving.

It didn't happen that way.

Lindsay and I were pulling the comforter across his top bunk, and Kendall was fixing his pillows when I heard Derek say, "Oh, golly, it's 2:00 P.M., and I'm supposed to be at a meeting *right now.*"

Nobody stopped to think. With a quick circle-of-family hug, he was gone. Out the door and down the hallway. It happened so fast. No final message. No prayer. I stood numbly in the middle of the room, but then I turned to look out his window . . . and . . . in that moment that will be etched in my mind forever, I watched him turn down that sidewalk and walk away from us. Alone.

My tears came then, and I knew I was not a bit good at this "letting go" stuff. And good-byes—even though they are part of God's plan—are wrenching. I felt a stabbing sense of separation.

Impulsively, I grabbed a sheet of paper off his desk and scribbled down three familiar family messages we'd tried to pass on to our children as they grew up: "Remember, Derek: (1) There's no *problem* so big you can't solve it; (2) we'll *always* love you; and (3) you are *never* alone. Love, Mom."

I tucked the paper under his pillow, and the four of us walked solemnly out to the car to begin our long journey home. I noted *Lesson #6: If you want to have a meaningful discussion or time of prayer, don't wait until the last minute, or it may not happen.*

I've heard families debate whether to drive their freshmen to college. "The good-bye is so much more difficult on the steps of a dormitory than in the comfort of our own home," one parent said. But we appreciated delivering Derek to school so we could visualize him in his room and on the campus. We also liked meeting his roommate and his parents and enjoyed helping him move in and get settled. And the trip gave us a chance to spend time together away from the routines and obligations that distract us at home.

Most of all, we drove Derek to college because that's what he wanted. We would not have gone if he had wanted to make the trek on his own.

Though we had a good time on our trip, not all families have the same experience. Some described bickering or sullen silences en route or just before the big good-bye. Even though parents realize that anger or irritation often covers the real fears of separation, that tension is not pleasant. Others complained of "feeling like we were in the way once we got to campus" because their son or daughter was distracted by other priorities.

Some parents appreciate the drive to campus as a good means of transition, a pocket of time to adjust and reflect. One mother of four claims she and her husband have made a tradition of driving their kids to college and then taking a few days alone together to "give full rein to our joy and grief." They spend hours rerunning that child's life, remarking on the growth and maturity in 18 short years.

I appreciated the drive home as a time to grieve. The hum of the tires on a smooth stretch of highway lulled me into a reflection on the passage of time. When the kids were little and I was young, time stood still. The thought of their leaving home was so distant that I had a silly notion it might never come.

Time also stood still during those exhausting moments when I had three small children under the age of five and all I wanted was a tiny space of time to myself, without all those appendages hanging off my arms and legs. I particularly remember one day when I stood in the checkout line of the supermarket, trying to corral the three cherubs who had been chasing each other up and down the aisles. I finally caught them and stuffed them into my grocery cart, where they were making their final assault on the gum and candy rack so conveniently placed at that narrow spot in the checkout line. I looked like a frustrated octopus trying to catch hold of six hands at once. Just then, a kindly looking grandmother wheeled in behind me.

"Enjoy these years, honey," she said with a smile. "They pass too quickly."

I thought she was loony at the time, but driving home from delivering Derek to college, I knew she was right. Time may stand still in the present, but when I look back over my shoulder, the years zoom by.

As we continued our journey toward home, the reality of the change began to sink deeper into me. Soon I would face the empty bedroom, the empty place at the dinner table, even the empty spot in the garage where he parked his bike. Was this pain partly my fault? Had I woven the threads of my life too tightly around the lives of my children? Had I sacrificed too much of myself and too many of my own interests through the years to go to soccer games or drive them to piano lessons or be there during homework hours?

Suddenly, the unfairness of it all hit me hard.

"Why, Lord?" I wailed silently, looking out the car window. "Why, if we do it the way You tell us to—sacrificing, pouring our lives into the lives of our children—why does it hurt so much when they go? Is pain the price we pay for doing it Your way?"

I seemed to hear an answer as gentle as a whisper: "Yes, My child, because love *costs*. It cost Me My Son."

Oh, what a simple but powerful truth! When we love the way God calls us to love, there are costs and sacrifices. To love deeply means we'll sometimes hurt deeply. That's the price of the kind of love God demands, and I knew, even in my suffering, that I wouldn't change a smidgen of my investment. The pain of loving well is a good pain. The grief is a good grief.

The thought so comforted me that I began to feel better. I looked over at Lynn, who'd been driving for the last few hours, patiently enduring and enabling my need for silence. Kendall and Lindsay had again retreated into their world of Walkmans in the backseat.

"What do you suppose people do when their children leave home?" I asked Lynn.

"Look out the window and you'll see," he said.

I looked, watching the oncoming traffic, and began to notice a whoosh, whoosh, whoosh as a steady stream of RV's passed with happy-looking, grandparent-type couples perched in the front seats. The sight reminded me of what my friend Kathy said she and her husband were going to do when their two girls left home: "We'll simply get an RV and travel back and forth between their houses. We'll park in the driveway, roll out the awning, pull out our lawn chairs, and tell them to go right on with their lives while we just sit and watch them."

The traveling nest sounds a whole lot better than the empty nest.

By the time we reached home late the next night, I realized some of my grief had been spent in the trip. I was ready to get back into a routine and tackle the adjustment to Derek's absence. But I found myself looking forward to seeing him again, because I can say one thing for sure: I like hellos better than good-byes.

Other Good-byes

I wondered if I'd get any better at good-byes with practice, but taking Lindsay to college a year later felt nearly as difficult for different reasons. A daughter leaving home poses a different kind of loss for a mother. Though Lindsay and I had our differences years earlier, her last year and summer at home were good. We'd grown close, and I greatly enjoyed her companionship.

Again we packed up the car, and this time we delivered two to college. Lindsay had to be on campus first, and as we neared our good-bye, I felt the same ache of anticipation. This time around, we knew the routine. We got to town a day early, helped her get familiar with the territory, and then moved her into the dorm the next morning. Together, we attended a combined parent-student orientation where the school exuberantly welcomed the freshmen, raining confetti down from the ceiling.

Then it was time to say good-bye. Lindsay walked us to the car, where we hugged and said farewell. "Let her walk away. Don't let her watch us drive away," whispered Derek, the veteran of one college good-bye. So we stood and waited while she walked away. She turned and waved once, and then she disappeared into the dorm. I watched with blurry eyes.

We drove away from the campus, and I started to deal with a familiar grief. I'd been through it before, which made it easier. And since the family structure had already changed permanently with Derek's leaving home, this leave-taking seemed less frightening and threatening. I knew from experience that this good-bye grief, though profound, was temporary. Some of it would pass.

We took Derek on to college and then started our long trek home. Kendall's reaction surprised me. With both Lindsay and Derek gone, she suddenly became an only child. Her world changed even more than ours. And the experience of being so physically close to her siblings in the car on the trip seemed to magnify the reality of their absence. After we said good-bye to Derek, she crawled in the backseat of the car, pulled a blanket around herself, and grieved quietly, sometimes crying, all the way home.

Watching her pain grieved me more than my own. Sometimes I crawled back to sit beside her, but soon I realized that parts of grief are private. They must be endured alone. By the time we got home, she seemed better. She unpacked her belongings, hung some of her clothes in Lindsay's closet, spread her things all around the bathroom she no longer needed to share, and changed the message on the answering machine, excluding Derek's and Lindsay's names. A few weeks later, I heard someone ask her how she felt about becoming an "only child."

"I felt sad and lonely at first, but then I found the good parts," she replied. "I like it now."

One Moment of Great Grief

Families tolerate and adjust to the reality of separation differently, but for many, there seems to be a particular moment when the grief is most realized. One mother painfully recalls that moment: "We moved Hillary into the dorm where she stayed, while we spent the night in a nearby motel. We were to say good-bye the next day. I thought I was fine, but I woke up at 3:00 A.M. and cried until 6:00. By the time we said good-bye at noon, I was okay."

Another mother recalls moving her son into his dorm, attending orientation sessions, and then saying good-bye at the car. As she started to drive away, he leaned his head in the window. "I don't think I belong here," he said pathetically. Those words haunted her all the way home. Grief can be endured when we believe our children are okay, but the pain seems almost unbearable when we fear they're unhappy. A couple of days later, she got a call from a son who sounded better.

One mother recalls that her great moment of grief came several days after her son went off to college. She stood in the grocery store staring at the boxes of cereal, and suddenly she realized she didn't need to buy his favorite kind anymore. She left the store in tears.

Dr. James Dobson described his moment of great grief for his Focus on the Family friends in a letter after his second child and only son left home, opening the door to the empty nest for him and his wife, Shirley. His moment struck while driving his son to the airport: "There I was, driving down the freeway when an unexpected wave of grief swept over me. I thought I couldn't stand to see him go. It was not that I dreaded or didn't look forward to what the future held. No, I mourned the end of an era—a precious time of my life when our children were young and their voices rang in the halls of our house."

The good-bye at gate 18 was tearful as he realized that although his son would be home periodically in years to come, "our relationship will not be the same. It might be even better, but it will certainly be different."

The Dobsons returned to a home that three hours earlier had been a whirlwind of activity. Now it seemed like a "monastery—a morgue—a museum." He sat on the floor of his son's bedroom, grieving and thinking about the meaning of such separations during our earthly journeys toward heaven.

> It is not merely the end of formal parenting that has shaken my world today. I grieve for the human condition itself. When Ryan boarded that plane in Los Angeles, I comprehended anew the brevity of life and the temporary nature of all things. As I sat on the floor in his room, I heard not only Ryan's voice but the voices of my mother and father who laughed and loved in that place. Now they are gone. One day Shirley and I will join them. First one and then the other. We are just "passing through" as the gospel songwriters used to say. All of life boils down to a series of happy "hellos" and sad "good-byes." Nothing is really permanent, not even the

relationships that blossom in a healthy home. In time, we must release our grip on everything we hold dear. King David said it best, "As for man, his days are as grass; as a flower of the field, so he flourisheth. For the wind passeth over it, and it is gone; and the place thereof shall know it no more." Yes, I felt the chilly breeze of change blowing through my home this morning and I understood its meaning.[1]

Time has not erased the poignancy of the moment of good-bye for us as parents or for Lindsay and Derek as freshmen. As we return to their campuses for subsequent good-byes, we always walk through the freshman dormitories as a sort of remembrance to that moment in our lives. For me, the experience is kind of like visiting my parents' graves. It gives me a focal point for remembering. It reminds me of a period of great grief and also gives me a sense of thankfulness to God that I have passed through—and endured—a major transition. I'm on the other side of a passage and have grown through the struggle because of God's faithfulness.

On our last fall visit to campus, Lindsay and I walked down the long hallway of her old freshman dorm on the afternoon of good-bye. Many parents had already left. Some doors were closed; others revealed roommates chatting and getting settled. Down toward the end, we came to an open door. Inside, I could hear a mother sniffling. She stood over an ironing board, alone in the room, working vigorously on a pile of clothes on the bed. We witnessed the scene for only a second, but I had a longing to return and give that mother a comforting hug. There she stood, hanging on to those last few tasks she could accomplish for her daughter, knowing that when she finished ironing, she finished her moment of usefulness, and finally she would have to say good-bye.

I wanted to tell her that the days and hours of anticipating the good-bye were worse than getting on with the business of living them. I wanted to tell her I understood the physical pain she felt—

as if the fibers that have bound you together are tearing apart—but that the moment of great grief doesn't last. In God's plan, suffering and grief often precede the coming of new life and a new beginning. That's what happened between Good Friday and Easter Sunday with His Son. That's part of His divine pattern in all of creation. Grief and suffering blossom into new life for those who love Him.

People say life will never be the same after a child leaves, and they're right. Life won't ever be the same, because it's not *supposed* to be the same. We have to let go of the old so we can let in something new. Life will be different. And better. For those who trust Him.

This is not a hopeless good-bye. It's a hope-*full* good-bye, part of God's plan for parents and children. Their going means we've done our jobs.

That's why our great grief can be good grief.

11

Home-Front Adjustments

*T*he best part of a family vacation is coming home.

We certainly felt that way as we pulled into our driveway well past midnight, completing the last leg of our first journey to deliver Derek to college nearly 1,500 miles away. Exhausted, we carried our suitcases into the house, quickly checked the mail, and looked through the stack of newspapers. To our horror, we read that a friend, a young man a few years older than Derek, had been killed in an accident.

I went to bed but couldn't sleep.

Some people compare the grief parents experience when a child leaves home to the grief parents feel when a child dies. They're not the same. Though there may be similarities in adjusting to the physical absence, the death of a child brings a different, much deeper pain, including the death of hope for that child's earthly future. When a child leaves home for college, parents feel a sense of loss in the child's going, but they are filled with great hope for the child's future.

During that first sleepless night at home, I put my grief into perspective and got up the next day, ready to start my journey through the transition of becoming a family of four instead of five. Gail Sheehy calls this kind of loss "making a major detachment" that feels like a "small death."[1]

As I look back over that period now, I realize I made the adjustment in my own style. I embraced the full range of feelings, slowly reached some places of growth and understanding, and finally emerged at the end of that first year with a sense of thankfulness for having made it through.

Though every family copes with the transition in its own way, there are some common responses, regardless of whether the child leaves home for school, the military, a job, or marriage. Most parents claim the reality of the absence catches them by surprise. "Where did the years go?" a dad wonders, waking up to the realization that his daughter is gone. "It seems you were here such a short time," another comments.

Most families enter the season of the emptying nest slowly, making adjustments to changes over a period of several years as children leave home one by one. And many parents joke that by the time the last one graduates, the first one is back home again. At any rate, most families have an opportunity to adjust slowly to the absence of children, and many claim the first is the hardest. With that absence, the family is forced out of the familiar mold it has lived within for 18 years or more. Subsequent changes seem less difficult. Others, however, claim the last is the most difficult.

Grieving

For the first few months after Derek left, our family felt like a body with an arm amputated. The loss was painful, and we all grieved. But eventually, we learned to compensate.

Grieving is an important step toward acceptance of a loss, and it's a process with many parts. In the beginning, I mainly felt sad, as if I had a puddle of "cry" within me that I couldn't quite tap into or drain. My tears spilled out at odd times: watching a coffee commercial on television where a son comes home from the Army and surprises his mother by brewing coffee in the kitchen early one morning, or seeing an older brother taking his younger sister's hand and leading her off to Sunday school. Sometimes I felt a gnawing need to weep for a life left behind me.

Another stage of grief is denial. At first, I saw our change as temporary and began living in wait of Derek's return, when we would be a family again. Obviously, I was denying the permanency of the change. When we got home from taking him to college, I circled December 18—the day he'd come home for Christmas—on the calendar with a red pen. I began living inside that circle of thinking. We would endure his absence until he returned. For the first time, I welcomed the sight of Christmas decorations in October. They made Derek's return more imminent.

I also missed seeing him. The grief caused by his physical absence surprised me. I longed to look at his face to assess how he was doing. I longed to see him talking with his new friends or walking across campus. I wanted to sit right next to a person in church who had visited him a week earlier. I hungered for a closeness, even secondhand.

During those first few weeks, I caught myself looking at the clock and wondering what he might be doing—eating, going to a movie, studying. I used to know those things. I grieved the loss of involvement in the dailyness of his life, and I missed knowing his routines.

I also experienced some guilt and regret, common parts of grieving. As I adjusted first to Derek's and then later to Lindsay's absence, I had moments of regret that we didn't pray more or encourage them to memorize more Scripture or read more books together. One day shortly after Lindsay left, I stood stretching in an aerobics class and noticed a young woman about Lindsay's age, moving with the obvious grace of one trained in ballet. Suddenly, I felt a stab of regret that I hadn't encouraged Lindsay to take ballet. My mother made me take ballet. How could I have forgotten ballet? What kind of mother would forget? Those silly ballet questions haunted me all during that class.

The grief over their going triggered the awareness of other, connected losses, such as the reality of aging. One autumn morning soon after Lindsay left for school, I hosted a breakfast meeting for a group of women. I rushed around, setting out cups, spoons, fresh fruit, and muffins. I carefully filled a 50-cup coffee maker with water and 25 huge scoops of coffee grounds, but in setting it on the counter, I tipped the whole thing over, filling the open drawers and cupboards with soggy coffee grounds and a zillion gallons of water. I wanted to cry. This was no mere accident. It was a preview of the kind of klutz I was becoming as I aged.

Then a woman showed up with the pitiful description of her mother's advancing Alzheimer's disease. I shook my head in sympathy—and fear, imagining myself following in her footsteps. After all, I knocked over coffeepots, sometimes forgot people's names, and could hardly read my own handwriting. The week before, I even left my groceries at the grocery store. The combination of losses—losing kids and losing my mind—seemed too much.

Denial, depression, and a desire to give up are all symptoms of grieving. So, finally, are acceptance and the emergence (or remembrance) of hope. "After you have suffered a little while, [Christ] will himself restore you and make you strong, firm and steadfast," Peter promised the early Christians in 1 Peter 5:10. Somewhere in the midst of grieving comes a ray of hope. In the dark nighttime sky, some stars begin to shine.

Solutions to Grieving

Focus on what's left, not what's lost. The year Derek left, I remember driving alone down a country road on a cold, dreary day in early November, thinking how the season and weather matched my mood. The last of the leaves had blown off the trees, leaving barren branches and a desolate landscape. Everything in nature reflected the loss of vitality that I felt. The fields had lost their green grass; the trees had lost their leaves; and I had lost my secure definition of *family*, which always meant five people living together in a home.

As I drove past the huge, barren cottonwood trees lining the road, something caught my eye. Wedged in the leafless branches of the trees were big nests, revealed only because the leaves were gone. That might not seem like such a big deal, but to me at that moment, it seemed a revelation. The loss of leaves revealed what was left in the branches, which I had hardly noticed, because I'd been focusing on what was lost. And what was left—those nests—was the best part!

When my child leaves home, what do I have left? I still have Jesus. I have my husband; our home; a growing, changing definition of *family;* friends; Christmas and a new year; hope; God's promises; prayer . . . and soon my drive down that country road turned into a celebration of thanksgiving. After that, I focused more on what I had left instead of what I had lost.

The mothers' prayer group. My friend Joyce organized a group of mothers to support each other and our college kids through a small prayer chain. In the fall, we got together once a month as we adjusted to the absence of our kids. Because of our shared understanding of the loss, we validated the importance of our feelings and gave each other permission to grieve. We learned that we don't get *over* the loss, we get *through* it, partly by walking alongside each other and talking through our responses.

Organizing a mothers' prayer support group was simple. The self-appointed leader invited eight mothers for coffee. We established our phone tree, made prayer requests, and spent time in prayer. Between meetings, we committed to pray regularly for our college kids' protection, friendships, and hunger for God, as well as for our own discernment as we entered the new phase of long-distance parenting. We stayed in touch by phone as prayer needs came up. Before final exams and Valentine's Day, each of us brought nine treats, signed cards, and put together care packages for our kids. This mothers' prayer group not only comforted me, but it also gave our college kids added prayer support in difficult times.

Praise and promise journal. I kept a journal of my journey through transition, especially noting some good things I discovered. For example, I didn't have to go to the grocery store so often; I faced fewer piles of clutter on the kitchen counter and fewer dishes in the dishwasher; I didn't find the car on "E" so often; I had fewer distractions and more time with Lynn; I had fewer school papers to read, sign, and send back.

I also recorded God's promises that helped me. When I needed to remember my sorrow would not last forever, I repeated, "Weeping may remain for a night, but rejoicing comes in the morning" (Ps. 30:5). When I wondered about God's bigger-picture plans for my life, I remembered, "For I know the plans I have for you, . . . plans to prosper you and not to harm you, plans to give you hope and a future" (Jer. 29:11). And when I needed to let go of the past and look toward the future, I noted, "I forget all that lies behind me and with hands outstretched to whatever lies ahead I go straight for the goal" (Phil. 3:13-14, Phillips).

Cleanup therapy. While grieving the absence of a child, I found great therapy in tackling a messy closet or cluttered room. Bringing a sense of order to something chaotic like a bureau drawer brought a sense of order to my up-and-down feelings. Getting organized gave me a comforting sense of readiness for the new season.

Creating closeness. I devised ways to create a sense of closeness to our faraway kids. I posted their class schedules near my desk so I knew where they were at 1:00 P.M. on Tuesdays and Thursdays. I sipped coffee out of mugs from their schools and kept their latest pictures near the phone. I learned the first year that if I kept their high-school graduation pictures near the phone, I froze them in time with that look. Now I keep their latest pictures close so that when I talk with them, I picture them as they look *now*.

Looking ahead. I kept adding to the list of things I want to do in the next season of life. I want to read every book on a list of classics I have. I want to take one class a year in *something*. I want to hike to the bottom of the Grand Canyon. Writing down these goals kept me looking beyond where I was to what's ahead.

The grieving process is normal and healthy, and we move through it more easily when we talk about our feelings instead of trying to act as though the loss doesn't matter. We're open about our feelings with God, our spouses, and supportive friends, but not necessarily with our college kids. "Let them know you miss them but that you're okay, so they don't feel responsible for your happiness or carry the burden of your pain too far," a friend advised wisely.

Facing Changes

People grieving a death often describe the first year as the most difficult, because they have to endure each annual event without the presence of their loved one. Similar challenges face a family with a son or daughter away at college—the first Thanksgiving, the first family birthday, the first family vacation minus one. Lindsay spent her first birthday away from home her freshman year. When I called a bakery to order a cake for her, my voice got all wobbly. *Oh, good grief,* I scolded myself, *you're crying on the phone long distance to a total stranger just because he asked what you want to say on the card.*

Family traditions are hard to change, and though parents have more flexibility and freedom when children leave home, they also have less predictability. We always spent Thanksgiving at home and invited other people, but with two away at college, our family of three faced the question of what we should do on Thanksgiving. We'd never asked ourselves that before.

Family meals change, too. When we got down to three family members, I filled the refrigerator with more bagels and yogurt, and I cooked less. We fell into a monotonous pattern of sitting at the kitchen counter and eating either pasta or baked chicken breasts.

"I'm so hungry for some *real* food," Kendall lamented one night. I knew what she meant—a casserole that baked slowly, smelled good when she came in the door from school, and provided leftovers for late-night snacks.

The next night, I made a huge enchilada casserole that did all those things.

The Empty Bedroom

Another adjustment is living with the empty bedroom. For some parents, walking by the door of that empty room is the most constant and painful reminder of the permanent change in the family. My friend Jeanne put some green plants in her daughter's room and opened the windows each morning "to bring a feeling of life to the emptiness."

Some parents have "room rituals," leaving the room exactly as the son or daughter left it or cleaning it thoroughly the day the child leaves, hoping for some of that cleanup therapy. I put off the thorough cleaning until just before they come home. There's great joy in changing sheets while anticipating their arrival.

Newspaper columnist Ellen Goodman wrote about the status of that empty bedroom in her home, vacated four years earlier by her daughter, who was away at college. The room and its teenage memorabilia were frozen at about age 15, according to Goodman, and felt melancholy, like a "waiting room that expects the return of a missing child, when in fact it is a young woman who comes home these days." Over the phone one day, the mother mentioned redecorating. The daughter objected.

"Do you want this room to remain a shrine to your adolescence forever?" the mother asked.

"Yes," the daughter answered with a laugh.

The mother hung up, knowing they were talking about more than interior decorating. They were talking about growing up and growing apart.

"When they go home, for a week or a summer," the mother later reflected, "they say it's hard for parents to acknowledge how much they've changed. But these young do not say—because they don't always know—the difficulty they have letting parents change, letting home change.

"How many people moving onto the shaky turf of independence want the security of knowing that they can go home again? How many want to believe that they can be children again? There is comfort in the idea that parents, like bedrooms, are freeze-framed in their old places, not demanding but available, always there in case of emergency."[2]

We filled one of our two empty bedrooms with Amy, a 27-year-old former baby-sitter who needed a place to live for a year, and the arrangement worked well all the way around. Kendall got an older sister again, we enjoyed having her as a temporary member of our family, and we felt thankful to be able to offer a space to someone who needed it.

Long-Distance Parenting

Long-distance parenting poses a new and confusing challenge. We don't accumulate much experience in this task through the years, and we feel a bit bewildered by it. As the father of one college student said, "This is the most difficult stage of parenting so far. Our financial investment is the highest, and our satisfaction—or feedback—is the lowest. We hardly hear from our son, and when he calls, we're not sure whether to merely listen, offer advice, or tell him what to do."

These feel like yo-yo years again as college kids go back and forth between needing us and not needing us. Sometimes their phone calls sound pitiful; sometimes they're too busy to talk. Sometimes they're full of news about their choice of classes for next semester and spring break plans; at other times, they can't make a decision about where to go to study.

Long distance, we're renegotiating the terms of our relationship.

"Each transition from one phase to the next," wrote psychoanalyst Judith Kestenberg, "presents a challenge to both parents and children to give up outdated forms of interactions and to adopt a new system of coexistence. The ability of a parent to meet his side of this challenge depends on his inner preparedness to accept the new image the child forms of him and to erect a new image of the child."[3]

If we respond to our almost-adults' needs at this stage of parenting, we allow that yo-yoing without putting too many expectations on them. We allowed our freshmen to call home when they needed. Sometimes that call came at two in the afternoon. Sometimes the call didn't come for more than a week as they explored both the dependence and the independence of this new, long-distance relationship.

Long-distance parenting depends heavily on phone calls and mail delivery. Calls can be wonderful—or difficult. We identified some as "dump" phone calls, when kids unload all their pressures onto the shoulders of sympathetic parents. Undoubtedly, the kids hang up and feel a great sense of relief, while the parents crawl away from the phone, carrying the burden of all those troubles. As the "dump receptors," we have to keep their problems in perspective and not allow them to become ours.

Phone conversations can also be difficult because we jump into them with no knowledge of the moods preceding them or the needs of the students.

"Mom, it's a beautiful Saturday afternoon, and I don't *feel* like studying," Lindsay moaned to me over the phone from her dorm recently.

That was all I needed to launch into a lecture on self-discipline. "Lots of life is having to do things we don't *feel* like doing," I started off. "I didn't *feel* like getting up when the alarm went off this morning, and I didn't *feel* like—"

"Mom, I just called to talk, not to hear a lecture," Lindsay interrupted.

Obviously, that conversation didn't go so well. Lindsay needed sympathy, and I needed to straighten out her life, because I have so few opportunities to do that. I reminded myself of Patsy Clairmont, mother and author, who said, "My kids don't realize I have the gift of advice." When they call home, they want a listener, not a lecturer.

Long-distance loving means communicating the message that the student is loved and missed and still an important member of the family. This is tangibly communicated through the mailbox. Our mothers' prayer group shared ideas about how to keep something in the mailbox, especially during that freshman year, when finding an envelope feels like touching home base. Here are some ideas that supplement the longer letters:

➤Keep a supply of prestamped postcards or picture postcards from the hometown area on hand for quick, one-liner messages.

➤Tape a stick of gum to an index card. ("I'm sticking with you today!")

➤Clip articles of interest from the newspaper, or send the sports section.

➤Send a few of the latest family photos with captions.

➤Send the church newsletter.

➤Send a tape you've enjoyed. Make a tape.

➤Have a little brother or sister or neighborhood child draw a picture.

➤Write some "Proverbs from Home," starting with Proverbs 32 (since the Bible stops at 31). This is a good way to tuck in some advice.

The apostle Paul mastered the art of long-distance loving by staying in touch with new Christians through letters. He knew what I'm learning: The written word is tangible, permanent, and meaningful. Letters give people something to hold on to. Though we may not get many letters from our kids, our mail to them maintains the home-base bond. Of course, they like care packages, too.

Long-distance worrying is a new part of parenting. I got pretty good at worrying while they lived at home, and I believed, in some mixed-up way, that my presence or closeness gave them a measure of protection. Judith Viorst expressed the same attitude:

> For many mothers do believe that their actual bodily presence stands between their children and all harm. It is, I confess, a belief that I used to share. I once (I know this sounds ludicrous) was positive that as long as I was right there, my sons couldn't choke to death on a piece of meat. Why? Because I knew that I would keep nagging them to take smaller bites and chew carefully, and because I also knew that if worse really came to worst, I would seize a knife and perform a tracheotomy. Like many mothers, I saw myself—and in some ways see myself still—as their guardian angel, their shield of invulnerability. And although I have had to let my sons explore more and more of this perilous world alone, I am haunted by the anxiety that they always will be at far greater risk without me.[4]

"Mom, we're climbing Mount Hood this weekend," Derek told me excitedly over the phone one Friday afternoon.

My brain, which easily forgets the names of my next-door neighbors, suddenly became like the scanner in a library subject index, bringing up on my screen every scary story I'd ever heard about accidents on Mount Hood. I especially remembered avalanches.

"Don't worry, Mom," Derek said, hearing my silence. "We're taking crampons and compasses and—"

"Oh, Derek," I moaned. He'd heard that worried voice before.

"Mom," he said quietly. "I need you not to be afraid . . . because that makes me feel afraid. Erik's father is going with us, and he knows what he's doing."

Derek was right. He didn't need to carry the burden of my fears up that mountain with him. Poised with the phone in my hand, I had a choice of responses about his adventure. I could ask, "Why in the world would you want to climb that mountain?" Or I could say, "I think you're courageous, and I know you'll handle it well."

By God's grace, I chose the latter, hung up, and started praying.

My worries should not confine my children's choices, so every time I hear they're going on a 1,000-mile road trip, camping in the mountains, or exploring the streets of a large city, I go back to the prayer of relinquishment and make the mental journey up Mount Moriah, praying for their protection and trusting God with the results.

College kids are smart, though, and they soon realize there are things you simply don't tell your mom. Then she doesn't worry. Maybe they're right.

Long-distance involvement is a tricky challenge of parenting that sometimes demands an instinctive response. When do we call a resident adviser, dean, or professor? When there is some information (personal, health, or academic) that will make a difference and that the student will not or cannot give. Parents call because they want the dean of students to be sure their son or daughter spends more time in the library. That's not appropriate. Parents call because there's been a death or a critical health issue in the family that they know the student will not divulge. That's appropriate. The guidelines here are fuzzy, as is much of parenting in this stage, but it seems appropriate to err on the side of giving too much information.

Short-Distance Parenting

Short-distance parenting aims at the child who leaves home for a job, marriage, or school in the same town or one nearby. In many ways, this parenting is similar to the long-distance kind: the adjustment to the yo-yo of being needed and not needed, the temptation to overworry simply because the child no longer lives at home, and the challenge of knowing when to get involved with an employer, professor, or friend. But the communication pattern is often different. For one thing, nearby kids can come home for visits often (or parents can visit them), and phone calls are free and easy. This creates a challenge in itself.

"When Mirian moved into a dorm across town, I vowed not to interfere. I kept my distance and always waited for her to call me," one mother said. "I thought that worked out well, but Mirian told us later she felt sad she never got any mail or care packages, which is true. I tried to give her long-distance space, but I didn't really act like a long-distant parent. I never thought to drop her a note or send a surprise box of cookies. None of her relatives did, either. They assumed that since she lived in town, she didn't need those letters, but she felt left out of that part of college, especially when everyone else got mail."

That same mother admitted that the joy of having her daughter go to college close by was the opportunity to have her friends over for Sunday dinners and Thanksgiving and Easter celebrations.

Another parent adopted a stricter policy to emphasize the independence of her in-town college student. "I told my son he couldn't come home for at least a month," this mother explained, "so he learned to adjust to his dorm and didn't give in to the temptation to run home."

I know a man who gave in to the temptation to take care of his daughter's every need when she moved into a dormitory across town. He picked her up and took her to the grocery store once or twice a week, and he sometimes acted as her late-night pizza delivery man. Now he looks back on all that with a sheepish grin, admitting his responses were excessive as he adjusted to her leaving home.

Another couple faced the challenge of parenting their college student who moved back home after a noisy and unsuccessful semester in the dorm. "Since high school, we haven't given him many rules—as long as he makes good choices—so he feels comfortable living at home. We try to pick our battles and stick with only important issues, so we don't tell him when to study or when to be in at night. Our rules are more general, like asking him to tell us whether he'll be here for dinner and asking for help in cleaning up around the house. Yet, these are the rules of respect we hope he'd live by in an apartment with a group of friends."

That same mother admits she sometimes bites her tongue on her instinctive responses to issues like appearance or girlfriends, "which is hard when he's here all the time." But in those cases, she stops herself and often goes on a walk with her husband to talk about her feelings: "He's calmer about these things than I am, and he helps me see when I need to back off."

Children who leave home for a job and an apartment face many of the same challenges of separation as one leaving for college, though their social schedules and context of friends are not the same as in a dormitory. One mother always informed her son of upcoming family events but made it clear he was under no obligation to attend. "We felt we walked a fine line. We didn't want to intrude, but we also didn't want him to feel left out. He appreciated that."

Mother's versus Father's Adjustment

Does the mother or the father have a harder time adjusting to kids' growing up and leaving home? The answer seems to depend mostly on their God-given personalities, though mothers generally are thought to be more feeling oriented. I've often heard this statement: "Mothers care about their children's *happiness;* fathers are concerned with their *success.*" Mothers seem tuned in to their children's gradual departure, and fathers seem more surprised by their absence. They may feel more regret, especially about being gone so much during the children's growing-up years.

"In the back of my mind, I always rationalized that the time would come when I could spend more time with them," one dad said. "But it never did. All of a sudden, they were gone."

I've always assumed that mothers who stay home with their children find the adjustment more difficult, but Ellen Goodman disagrees:

> A long time ago, I thought that mothers who also had work that engaged their time and energy might avoid the cliché of an empty-nest syndrome. . . . Now I doubt it.
>
> Those of us who have worked two shifts, lived two roles, have no less investment in our identity as parents, no less connection to our children. No less love. No less sense of loss.
>
> Tomorrow, for the first time in 18 years, the part of my brain that is always calculating time—school time, work time, dinner time—can let go of its stopwatch. The part of me that is attuned to a child's schedule and needs as it is to a baby's cry in the night will no longer be operative. I don't know how easy it will be to unplug.[5]

For almost two years, I kept "unplugging" responses as I adjusted to first Derek's and then Lindsay's absence. Transitions are tough, with spots of growth along the way. For me, the first Thanksgiving without Derek triggered such a moment of growth. For years, I'd dreaded the thought of that first family holiday without him. His empty place at our Thanksgiving table would symbolize the permanent change in our family structure. Yet, by the end of the day, I'd gained an understanding that still helps me through family transitions.

I felt mad at God that Thanksgiving morning.

"When You got the idea of *connecting* people in families, did You know how hard it would be to *disconnect* after kids grow up and go away?" I asked, stuffing another fistful of dressing into the turkey.

"Families belong *together* on Thanksgiving," I continued to complain, "and we all feel totally out of whack around here."

I finished stuffing the turkey and slid it into the oven, slamming the door.

Soon 13-year-old Kendall walked into the kitchen.

"Sure doesn't look much like Thanksgiving around here yet," she observed, noticing only the bare essentials set out on the table. "We need some decorations."

With that, she began opening drawers and randomly pulling out mismatched candles, a couple of bowls, and even some tin cookie cutters. She liked the challenge of creating something out of nearly nothing. I watched curiously as she began piling fruit in a silver bowl and grouping candles together on the table. Then she stood back and looked at the cookie cutters still on the counter.

"How about a cookie-cutter family?" she suggested, pulling out five figures and reaching for some dental floss to tie them together. With the help of a coat-hanger frame, she created an instant, whimsical family mobile, which she hung in the window over the dining room table. The tin figures dazzled in the sunlight as they bounced around crazily.

"We look a little wobbly, but at least we're still connected," she said with a grin. "I'm going to get dressed."

As I started scrubbing potatoes, I kept looking back at the cookie-cutter mobile and thinking of Kendall's words. More than the empty place at the table, the mobile symbolized our family in transition. Derek had moved to a different place, which caused the rest of us to feel a little wobbly and out of whack. But eventually, we'd all settle down and adjust to the new configuration. Most important, in spite of the new positions, we remained connected as a family.

I opened the oven door to baste the turkey and thanked God for this comforting new symbol of a family in transition—changing shape but staying connected.

That cookie-cutter mobile still hangs in our window.

12

Freshman Disorientation

"*I*'ll never forget the first few days of my freshman year," Lindsay told us recently. "After I said good-bye to you, I had to walk back into that dorm and start acting happy. Nobody knew anybody, and the kids were making up their minds about each other, so I wanted to be the kind of person other people would like. Even my two roommates didn't know whether I was friendly or weird or stuck-up or moody. I had to start from zero. I felt scared and unsure of myself, but I tried to act confident—like I had it all together.

"That insecurity lasted for months. My whole freshman year seemed like an exhausting roller coaster of highs and lows. Sometimes I felt like I needed a good cry, but of course, I didn't dare. Not until I got sick—then I cried and cried and longed to be home."

Derek's freshman memories are even worse—so bad, in fact, that I hesitate to describe them. I do so with his permission, however, because he learned some valuable lessons from the struggles of those first few days. After saying good-bye to us, he went off to a meeting and then returned to his dorm to get ready for the freshman camping trip, a traditional part of the student orientation activities. As he gathered his diabetic supplies, he discovered with dismay that he was missing a certain kind of insulin. He must have left it at home in the haste of packing. He panicked as he faced his worst fear—coping with a diabetic problem totally on his own.

Then he remembered the first line of the note he'd found on his bed, and he began repeating it to himself: "There's no problem so big you can't solve it." He paused and took stock. He needed to find the right kind of insulin immediately, but he also needed to appear independent and didn't want to ask for help. So he checked the phone book, climbed on his bike, and started going from pharmacy to pharmacy, asking for directions as he went. He finally found the right insulin at a hospital emergency room and returned in time to get on the bus for the camping trip.

While on that trip, he suffered a diabetic reaction early one morning and wandered off in the woods by himself. Other people saw him go and assumed he wanted to be alone. Though he had nearly lost consciousness, by the grace of God (he doesn't remember this), he reached for the candy he always carries in his pocket. When he regained a sense of awareness, he found himself standing alone on the edge of a cliff.

When he returned to campus, he came down with a ferocious case of pinkeye, which not only added to an already self-conscious freshman's worries about appearances, but also confined him to his room for two days while the rest of the new students socialized at orientation activities.

On the first day of classes, Derek suffered another severe diabetic reaction. His roommate, Erik, finally roused him out of bed and assumed he was on his way to the bathroom. But instead, Derek, wearing only his underwear, went out the front door and wandered around in front of the dormitory, just as all the other students were rushing off to class. Erik, who was beginning to catch on to the symptoms of Derek's reactions, found him and gave him some juice. Derek "came to" with a horrifying realization of what he'd just done.

"I think I should transfer," he told me quietly on the phone that afternoon. "I'm so embarrassed." He sounded so broken.

I encouraged him, and then I encouraged his dear and patient roommate. "If you ever find Derek unconscious or come up against a problem you can't handle, just call 911," I told Erik. Though we'd never faced such problems in ten years of living with diabetes at home, I knew the accumulation of reactions and stress might be taking its toll.

Sure enough, the very next morning, Erik found Derek totally unconscious. Erik called 911, and paramedics carried Derek out of the dormitory on a stretcher. We all hit rock bottom that day. Lynn and I tried to do our best at long-distance parenting, realizing our own fears might destroy what little courage Derek had left. As we stayed in close contact with his doctor, we agreed he could pull through these crises by himself. To fly out there or demand he come home might forever jeopardize his confidence in coping alone.

Lynn and I, along with a close group of supportive friends, spent lots of time in prayer during those next few days. Within a week, Derek had achieved physical stability and gained a permanent sense of confidence, knowing he had successfully conquered one of his greatest fears. We praised God.

Derek gave me permission to tell this story because he hopes others will learn from it. This is his advice: *"First, be who you are.* I'm a diabetic, and I shouldn't let self-consciousness keep me from being who I am or telling others about myself. *Also, ask for help when you need it.* I didn't, because I wanted to appear as if I could handle everything myself, but I should have asked for help that first day when I needed to find the right insulin. And *don't forget what you've learned in the past.* I kept repeating those three messages I've heard since childhood: 'There's no problem so big you can't solve it, you are never alone, and we'll always love you.' They helped me. Finally, *no matter how bad things seem, don't give up. They will get better.* That first week, I felt like some weird wimp, but as soon as other people heard the truth, they were really nice. In a way, we were all in the same boat, self-conscious and afraid for different reasons."

His experience gave us a crash course in long-distance parenting. We learned that even the best preparation may not be enough during those first freshman weeks. Derek had been in charge of his diabetic care in high school, even purchasing his own supplies to prepare him for the independence of leaving home. But that still did not protect him from having problems.

We also learned that parents sometimes have to act on instincts, even when that action doesn't fit the "rule." We blamed ourselves for some of Derek's problems, because for fear of interfering, we didn't give his roommate or resident adviser (RA) more information about his diabetes. We were advised that parents should let their kids take responsibility for telling others about their diabetes. In principle we agreed, but we felt uneasy because Derek tends to be shy about telling others.

And finally, we learned to repeat the parents' prayer of relinquishment. After we contacted Derek's doctor and did all we could, we had to relinquish Derek and the circumstances and outcome to the Lord, trusting His sovereignty and sufficiency.

As both Derek and Lindsay look back at the beginning of their freshman years, their difficult memories all run together. "When I was living it, I took one day at a time and didn't think so much about it," Lindsay remembers. "But when I look back, I see one big blob of adjustments to being on my own away from home, making new friends and facing all the new academic challenges. It was stressful sometimes, but I sure grew up."

The freshman year—or any first year away from home—probably

represents the biggest change a person makes in an entire lifetime. Marriage is another huge adjustment, but at least a person faces those challenges with a loving, supportive partner. During the freshman year, especially at the beginning, students can feel very much alone. They have to rely on all the personal resources acquired during the seed planting and root building of their earlier years. We parents have to relinquish and trust as we respond to their feelings from a distance, more like observers and encouragers than participants. We pray they know where to turn for strength.

In *Necessary Losses*, Judith Viorst described the fearful vulnerabilities of the freshman year:

> Going away to college is a time when many shaky selves will falter. Unbuttressed by family and friends, there are boys and girls who will turn to themselves and find . . . nothing there. The college counseling services are filled with students whose separation anxieties are being masked by desperate escapes from pain. And while most of these students are hardy enough to survive their struggles with separation anxiety, some of them may sink beneath their damaging and sometimes deadly solutions.[1]

Those solutions include every parent's worst fears: taking drugs and alcohol; getting involved with a cultic group that replaces familial security; or forming other dependent relationships in which another person becomes a parent substitute. Kids leaving home need strength at the time of separation. We hope that strength comes from knowing that "apart from God, I can do nothing," and "with Him all things are possible." The truth of God's promises grows stronger through the struggles of the freshman year. The following pages describe some of those common struggles.

Search for Identity

All freshmen face the same overwhelming challenges Lindsay and Derek faced: "In high school, I asked, 'Who am I?' but I toyed with answers within the context of family and friends—within the expectations of being a son or daughter or good friend. Here, nobody knows me. I face a new freedom where there are no boundaries, labels, or histories. That's kind of frightening—and kind of exciting."

Gail Sheehy, in *Passages,* defined "Pulling Up Roots" as the first passage to adult life, when people begin to separate out their individuality from their parents' and to leave the security of home. This usually occurs between the ages of 18 and 22. Seeking an identity is important in the Pulling Up Roots passage: "The tasks of this passage are to locate ourselves in a peer group role, a sex role, an anticipated occupation, an ideology or world view. As a result we gather the impetus to leave home physically and the identity to *begin* leaving home emotionally."[2]

Seeking this identity with total freedom sometimes results in major changes in the way a student looks or acts, or in the groups joined or the type of friends chosen—sometimes even in a name change. Again for the parent-observer, these personality changes are bewildering. I felt encouraged by a college dean who said that "most college kids go through three or four personality changes before emerging as the person they will become—which usually is pretty close to a reflection of the parents' values."

As Gail Sheehy wrote, "A stormy passage through the Pulling Up Roots years will probably facilitate the normal progression of the adult life cycle. If one doesn't have an identity crisis at this point, it will erupt during a later transition, when the penalties may be harder to bear."[3]

Unlimited Freedom

Suddenly, during the first few days of being away from home, the realization of total freedom hits young people. *Nobody* knows if they change their sheets, study, or come in late at night. *Nobody* knows where they're going or what they're doing. *Nobody* even asks! The freedom is intoxicating. Then the frightening flip side of that freedom hits: *Does anybody care?*

Parents may give a high-school senior a lot of freedom, but as long as that senior lives at home, there's a built-in structure of accountability. Most colleges don't have such accountability systems—and don't want them. They have some rules (e.g., you can't cheat on tests and must maintain a certain grade point average to stay in school), but colleges don't want to replace an authoritarian figure, because they want the students to realize they're in charge of themselves.

The journey toward that mature accountability begins in high school, but it becomes more real when the young person leaves home and has the freedom to make more choices. Such choices may cause a struggle that Sheehy refers to as "breaking away from the inner custodian." The inner custodian is the voice of the parent that protects and guides us through childhood. When a child leaves home, he or she has the option of listening or not listening to that voice or replacing some of those messages with newly formed messages.

Judith Viorst wrote in *Necessary Losses,* "In building a life of our own, we challenge our family's myths and roles—and of course, we challenge the rigid rules of childhood. For leaving home will not become an emotional reality until we stop seeing the world through our parents' eyes."[4]

Most freshmen arrive at a moment when they realize they're released from many of those parental restrictions and messages, and that's when they begin to build their own systems into their lives: *I'm studying this afternoon, not because someone told me to but because I want and need to.* This mature self-discipline is the goal, according to the president of a Christian college: "If we were interested in simply controlling the behavior of our students, we would use a system similar to that of a police force or the courts. But we want our students to grow—spiritually, academically, and relationally."

He went on to define that relational growth: "We see many of our college students move from *dependence* (usually upon parents) to *independence* (almost a rebellious time of no accountability and breaking away), and finally to *interdependence*, which is the healthy goal of mature relationships. At that point, they have achieved a balance between being able to act independently and recognizing a need and desire for a connection to others."

Roommates

Roommates are an integral part of the freshman experience. A compatible roommate makes life easier; a difficult roommate makes life miserable. Most fall somewhere in between. No matter the relationship, the challenge of learning to live with a roommate becomes one of the greatest lessons of the freshman year.

"We're raised to be pretty selfish," says the dean of women at a Christian college. "Most freshmen have their own bedrooms at home. Now they have to share their space and compromise about their tastes in music, study habits, neatness, friends visiting, and lights on or off. No matter how well roommates get along, they will be forced to work out their differences, a coping skill that will help them for the rest of their lives."

Some college kids are assertive and have no trouble verbalizing their needs and clearly defining their boundaries to a roommate. Others are more compliant and try to overlook the little irritations instead of saying something about them. As one freshman explained, "That's the way I was raised, to put other people's needs first." But eventually, as the late-night visitors keep talking or the borrowed clothes are returned wrinkled and dirty, the compliant one finally explodes with an accumulation of unaddressed irritations. That's when parents often get a phone call of distress.

"I've had it with Mr. Inconsiderate!" one freshman told his parents.

The best we can do is to listen, acknowledge their feelings, and then offer suggestions about how to handle conflicts—if they're willing to listen. The first step is to check our own responses, recognizing that our instinctive reaction is likely to be loyally protective and also irritated with any person who treats our children unjustly. We are no help to them if we're angry. Our goal is to improve the situation, not fan the flames.

The second step is to help them clarify the conflict and separate the important from the unimportant—also what can be changed from what can't. What's the real problem? Irritations like the way they eat popcorn are small. Frequent late-night visitors are bigger problems.

When an irritating habit becomes a pattern, it needs to be addressed. Turning the other cheek is biblical, but we have only two cheeks. One late-night visitor might be overlooked. When such visitors become the norm, the subject needs to be discussed.

A third step is to clarify the way two people can discuss their differences. *Confronting* is a currently popular term, even in Christian circles, but the word sounds combative rather than compassionate. The motive in discussing a conflict is not combative or revengeful; it's not to dump out a bunch of angry feelings or pent-up frustrations. The motive is to repair and improve the relationship, to work out differences so the relationship can grow stronger rather than deteriorate because of unresolved issues. Jesus talks about "making peace with your brother" or "reconciling with your brother." The aim is to "speak the truth in love" for the purpose of building the relationship.

Some other guidelines include these: Don't speak in the heat of anger, but wait for a calmer, more rational moment. Use "I" messages rather than the more combative "You always . . ." Listen to the other person's side of the story, and be ready to compromise.

An example might be:

"Hillary, could we talk about something that's been bothering me? You're my roommate, and I care about you and want our friendship to keep growing. But lately, I've been feeling unimportant to you, because you allow your friends to keep coming in to visit after

I'm asleep, which wakes me up. I know you don't have a class until ten, but I have an eight o'clock, so I have to get up early. Do you have any suggestions for how we could work this out?"

I have to confess that my son gagged when he read that example. "That sounds like my high-school counselor teaching us how to communicate," he said. "It's probably the right way to do it, but guys don't talk that way." He couldn't come up with a better example, however.

Roommates don't have to be best friends, but they should be able to communicate, compromise, and be considerate of each other. If a person continues to have serious differences with a roommate, it's time to ask for help, first from an RA and then from someone in the housing department. Paul and Barnabas split up when their differences could not be settled. They were good people, but they served more effectively apart than together. They agreed to disagree. Sometimes roommates split up, but not before every effort has been made to work out the differences. The experience provides valuable practice in learning to communicate.

Homesickness

Feeling homesick, especially for freshmen, is painful and predictable, but it usually doesn't last long. It isn't something I wished on our college freshmen, but I expected it. You can't be part of a close family without sometimes missing that family after you leave, especially when college life gets a little tough, tiring, or impersonal. Homesickness can strike swiftly and feel debilitating, bringing on a wave of depression.

Kids who live close enough can go home once in a while to sleep in their own beds, have a quick dinner, attend a family celebration, or do a load of laundry, which gets their "home batteries" recharged. But for those who can't go home until Thanksgiving or Christmas, the pangs of homesickness are stronger, and those first few months can feel like a long stretch.

The worst cases of homesickness result in the vow that "I'm coming home" or "I'm going to transfer." Some students do, but many perfectly good colleges are left and lost in the emotional challenge of learning to live away from home. The college isn't the problem so much as the difficulty the freshman is having in making the adjustment.

My friend Barb got a phone call from her freshman daughter on the East Coast. "I don't think I belong here, Mom," the daughter said. "The kids drink a lot, which makes me wonder if I have to drink to fit in. And that makes me wonder if I know who I am anymore, and maybe I should drop out of school."

Wisely, my friend listened sympathetically and then said, "We'll talk about transferring after you finish the year out."

One week later, her daughter was fine.

Another freshman attending a Christian school phoned home and said she wanted to transfer because "at this school, you need to bring your own friends."

Campus administrators anticipate the problem of homesickness and know how to deal with it. Resident advisers in the freshman dorms at Derek's school put together a program called "Long-Distance Relationships" that focuses on healthy ways to live with the pain of separation from home and friends. Discussing feelings in small groups is one important way. When a freshman girl talked of missing her dog, others groaned sympathetically, and she felt better. The RAs also encourage freshmen to get involved in activities that create new friendships. Most colleges put all freshmen together in dormitories because they have similar needs and form close bonds quickly.

I remember a phone call from Lindsay a few weeks after school started. Though she had experienced some homesickness, she talked about her new friendships. "We're all getting so close," she reported enthusiastically. "Last night we agreed to be in each other's weddings!"

Homesickness usually gets the worst when a freshman gets sick for the first time. Suffering through the flu or a cold in a dorm room makes a 19-year-old feel like a child who's a million miles from home. It's a lonely experience that fills a fragile freshman with self-pity and wrenches the heart of a mother.

The phone rang at our house early one October morning, and I hardly recognized Lindsay's voice on the other end. I knew she'd had tonsillitis, but in the middle of the night, her tonsils had swollen so that she could hardly breathe or swallow. She felt as if she were suffocating, and she cried all night. She was afraid, and so was I. I immediately called her resident director, a woman who rushed Lindsay to a doctor. It was a rock-bottom day for Lindsay and for me, but she endured. Most freshmen have at least one rock-bottom memory.

Traditionally, mid-October is a difficult time for students. The exciting newness has worn off. The lack of privacy is wearing. So is the roommate. The first round of midterms is coming up. The weather's getting colder, and Thanksgiving vacation seems a long way off.

One mid-October, I sent Lindsay an article from *Seventeen* magazine called "Mom-Sick" that comforted us both. It started out this way: "I miss my mom. There, I've said it. One small sentiment that has more power to ravage a college girl's reputation than admitting she watches *The Bugs Bunny & Tweety Show* faithfully every Saturday morning." In the confusing freedom of college, that girl admitted she missed her mom because "she knows *me* better than anyone in the world."[5]

Communication Home

Modern technology narrows the distance when kids go away to college. That's good news and bad news. The good news is that long-distance calls are more economical than they used to be. When I went away to college 30 years ago, the phone was down the hall somewhere, and calls home were reserved for special occasions and emergencies. And no matter what, I always waited for the cheaper night rates to call. For our college kids, however, phoning home is the main form of communication, and our "phone home card" enables them to call at any time of day. "The sound of your mother's voice helps when you're feeling down," Lindsay admits.

The bad news is that we hardly ever get those great, descriptive letters anymore that become precious keepsake diaries of the journey through the freshman year. I still have mine because my mother saved them. Most college kids hardly ever write home now. One father lamented that he sent his heir apparent off to college with a bunch of 25-cent stamps that went out of date before he used one. About twice a year, I get an obligatory letter from our college kids that starts off with "Here's one for the scrapbook."

Parents generally get that one missive I call the absence-makes-the-heart-grow-fonder letter of appreciation. It's usually written in a sentimental, homesick moment when the freshman fully realizes the value of those parents he or she didn't care much about in high school. "Thanks for giving me up, Dad, but never giving up on me," wrote a son to his father. Those "I love you" letters are keepers for sure.

The invention of voice mail and answering machines adds another dimension to communication between home and school. "Please just call and leave a message once in a while," Derek asked. "I like coming back to my room and hearing your voice unexpectedly."

This easy-access communication has a couple of drawbacks. One is the "dump" call mentioned earlier, when the freshman calls home in a down moment and dumps all the troubles onto the parents.

Sometimes during these calls, I assume I can fix those problems. Derek called recently and described some discouragements. I suggested all sorts of solutions, quoted some Scriptures, and kept talking, determined to make him feel better before we hung up.

"Mom," he finally said, "you don't always have to fix it. Sometimes I just need you to listen."

"Oh," I said.

Easy-access phone communication can also result in phone

bills that "could buy a plane ticket home," Lynn claims. Our kids rarely call home more than once a week now, and I'm trying to cut down on the length of our conversations (which Lynn assures me I don't do well).

On the other end of the scale, communication can become too infrequent. "If you haven't heard from your student for several weeks," we were told at orientation, "write a note saying that you know the student has been working hard, so here's a $100 bill to spend. Of course, don't include any money. You'll hear from your child quickly!" A lack of communication might come from a reluctance to give bad news. Here's an example of such a letter from a college coed:

> Dear Mom & Dad:
>
> I am sorry I haven't written for so long, but I lost everything the night that demonstrators burned the dormitory down. I am out of the hospital now, and the doctor says my eyesight should return to normal soon. The wonderful boy Bill who rescued me from the fire offered to let me share his apartment. I accepted, and . . . you always said you wanted a grandchild, so . . .
>
> Love, Mary
>
> P.S. Please disregard the above. There was no fire. I haven't been in the hospital. I'm not pregnant and don't even have a boyfriend. But I did get a D in French and an F in Western Civilization, and I wanted you to receive this news in the proper perspective.

Stress

Whether it's homesickness, problems with a roommate, or the overwhelming load of academics, college kids often complain of stress, especially in their freshman year, before they learn how to handle it. Academic stress is at the top of the list, because the pressure is so constant. "There's always another midterm or paper due or book to read. I never feel like I finish," they often complain. "And getting good grades in college is much harder than in high school."

One mother, intrigued with those frequent conversations about stress, asked her daughters' friends to offer their tips on how to beat the stress after their freshman years at colleges all around the country. Here are some of their stress busters:

- Work out at the gym or go for a bike ride or jog—alone!
- Take a long car ride, playing a tape of great music.
- Call home and cry.
- Dress up like ninjas, and take popcorn to random people on another floor.
- Watch a sad movie and have a good cry.
- Get organized and make to-do lists.
- Take a nap.
- Call friends at home

Dorm Food

Complaining about dorm food is nearly as common as complaining about academic pressures and stress. I hardly ever use that famous parental line: "You should have seen it in my day. I had to walk three miles to school in the snow—barefooted." But when it comes to complaints about dorm food, I can emphatically say, "You should have seen it in my day!"

Dormitory cafeterias today include salad bars, potato bars, pasta bars, juice bars, and ice-cream sundae bars. That's a huge improvement over the creamed chipped beef on biscuits or kettle-of-something-mushy-that-stewed-for-hours that I often got in college. And we had no choices! One plate, one line, one scoop of whatever. Today, students have choices. At some schools, they're encouraged to "graze" (nibble their way through the line several times if they choose), and the fare is much healthier. (The University of Colorado even serves tofu lasagna!) Colleges are trying to meet students' changing tastes and eating habits, but the kids still complain the food is greasy and gross, mostly because they get tired of it.

Food symbolizes comfort and nurturing for some freshmen. For others, it represents one small area of control in the midst of a seemingly out-of-control life. The first situation can result in the weight gain known as the "freshman 15." The latter can lead to eating disorders such as anorexia and bulimia, which may require help beyond a parent's ability. Most colleges offer that help these days.

As parents, we need to listen to our kids who are struggling with the challenges of living away from home for the first time. We need to sort out the serious problems from the normal complaints and offer them sympathy, encouragement, and sometimes a bit of humor so they don't take themselves too seriously.

Billy Graham wrote in *Hope for the Troubled Heart,* "A keen sense of humor helps us to overlook the unbecoming, understand the unconventional, tolerate the unpleasant, overcome the unexpected, and outlast the unbearable."[6]

That sounds like the perfect prescription for freshman disorientation.

13

First Visits Home

*W*e burst through the mechanical doors and stepped from the frigid December night into the warm hustle and bustle of a crowded airport at Christmastime. We were a family minus one headed for a reunion on concourse B at precisely 10:34 P.M. Jittery with excitement, we checked the TV monitor for the gate and updated arrival time.

"Oh, no!" Kendall moaned. "It's going to be late."

After we'd endured Derek's absence for four months, you'd think we could stand a half-hour delay, but we all felt disappointed. All day, I'd been looking at the clock. *He's on his way to the airport. He's checking in. He's in the air.* Oh, how I longed for my first glimpse of that absent child, and now every minute mattered.

Still, there's no changing airline schedules, so we walked around the airport, watching other reunions and sweetening our own anticipation. Airports are happy places at Christmas.

181

Finally, it was time, and we all stood together on tiptoes at the gate, anxiously scanning the sea of faces that started coming through the walkway connecting the plane to the terminal.

Suddenly, we spotted him as he turned the corner, tall and grinning, a face above the others.

"There he is!" we all said at once.

Soon he stood before us, and for the briefest moment, I could see the changes in his face, a little less boy and a little more man. Surely, I recognized those changes only because I'd been deprived of seeing him for so long. When I'm around our kids every day, I hardly notice the subtle signs of growing up. They become obvious only after an absence. Yet almost as quickly, I absorbed those changes, and his new, grown-up face looked "regular" to me again.

We all hugged and walked together back down the concourse, barely knowing what to say in the reality of this long-anticipated moment. We retrieved his luggage and headed for the car, chatting about everything from the weather in Washington to the difficulty of his last final exam.

When we got home, Derek walked around the house slowly, looking at a familiar picture of the mountains in the hallway, touching the crèche on the table in the living room, standing silently before the Christmas tree, then finally carrying his suitcase and backpack to his bedroom. He came back a few minutes later, grinning.

"What's to eat?" he asked, opening the refrigerator door.

"How about tortillas and melted cheese?" I suggested.

As he sat at the kitchen counter, savoring his favorite late-night snack, he looked around again. "It's good to be home, Mom," he said.

That night I slept well, because a mother's great joy is knowing that each bed in the house is filled with the right person, probably like the mother hen who clucks happily after gathering in all her chicks. As a friend of mine said when her oldest returned home for his first visit, "I feel more complete when Tyler's home."

I nodded knowingly, but I wondered if feeling that way is dangerously wrong or absolutely, instinctively right.

The next morning was Sunday, and I got up early to make apple flapjacks. We all went off to church smelling like the Griddle Family. I loved it.

Unrealistic Expectations

The hardest thing about that first visit home is the unrealistic expectations we're apt to build about the joy of being together again. In our minds, we see ourselves picking up right where we left off or getting along even better. The fact is, however, that both parents and children have undergone changes, and the adjustment to being together again takes time. Often the most obvious changes are in appearance, which we notice immediately.

One mother and father drove to the airport to pick up their daughter. It was her first visit home. In the car on the way there, they promised each other they wouldn't comment on any changes, especially in her appearance. As they walked down the concourse, someone sort of familiar started coming toward them. *It's Jennifer,* they realized, except she looked so different, with cropped hair, pale skin, bright red lipstick, and strange clothing—a somber, mismatched, layered look.

"Don't say anything about her clothes," the father said under his breath.

"I'm not going to say anything about her clothes," the mother kept repeating as they walked quickly toward each other, smiling.

The closer they got, the less Jennifer looked like the daughter they knew. Finally, as they embraced, the mother blurted out, "Where on earth did you get those clothes?"

Sometimes the words seem to come out of our mouths uncontrollably. Even when we know what we should say. Even when we've vowed there are things we won't say. The powerful emotions of parenting override our rational thinking and cause us to say or do what we know isn't right.

Another mother handled a similar challenge a little better. All the way to the airport, she vowed not to say anything judgmental and decided *"That's interesting"* would be a safe comment. She stood at the gate, waiting for her compliant, short-haired son who'd gone off to college four months earlier wearing mostly T-shirts and blue jeans.

That same son got off the plane, his hair in a ponytail, wearing Army fatigues and carrying a backpack over his shoulder.

"Hi, Mom, how do you like my hair?" he asked with a grin, hugging her.

"Interesting," she said with a forced smile. "Let's go get your luggage."

"I didn't bring any luggage."

"Oh . . . *that's interesting,"* she said.

"I thought that if we washed these clothes, they'd be fine for most of vacation."

By the time they got to the car, she'd heard lots of "interesting" comments.

We also build unrealistic expectations about how quickly things will be just as they used to be. But they probably *won't* be just the way they were before, and if they come anywhere close, the transition will take time. Parents and children need time to get used to each other again after a long separation.

On a different scale but based on the same principle, prisoners of war go through a debriefing period and quiet transition time to prepare them to slowly reenter the world they left. Kids reenter a vastly different zone when they go from dorm life to family life in a few hours. Derek responded quietly, almost as if he were in shock, and when we gave him his space, he warmed up. We've learned not to bombard a returning college student with questions on the way home from the airport, or even in the first 24 hours.

Home Rules

Talking about rules and issues helps everyone adjust to being back together. Parents and college kids often have different agendas and expectations, and unless those differences are communicated and compromised with patience, the vacation can be filled with disappointment and resentment. Consider their college environment. They've been used to living with little accountability. They leave their dorm rooms without telling anyone where they're going or when they'll be back. With flexible dining hours, they eat when they want, or they don't eat at all. They may have an understanding with their roommates that they're not sociable before noon, and the roommates don't care. In short, their habits in college are not "family friendly," and sometimes the readjustment period requires flexibility.

"At 10:30 one night, my parents were on their way to bed, and I told them I was going out," a freshman said after the first week home. "My mom tried to talk me out of it because it was too late. She didn't understand that in college, our evenings *begin* about 10:30."

"I expect at least the same thoughtfulness from my college kids home on vacation that I do from a guest in my home," one mother told me. "I like to know about when they'll be home, and I expect them *not* to leave their sweaty gym clothes on the kitchen table. It's not a bunch of control issues; it's simple consideration for the people with whom you live."

At the beginning of vacations, especially Christmas vacation, with a lot going on, it helps to talk about agendas and family obligations (though that word is deadly!), including visits to grandparents, invitations to family parties, and church programs.

Curfews call for compromise. Since they had none in college, we didn't give our college kids curfews at home. But I told them I'd like to know about when they'd be home so I could plan meals and not worry.

On their first visit home, they are bound to test some of the values and limits of their new independence, just to assure themselves (and us) they've made a break. For some, it may mean going out at 10:30 at night. For others, it may be a whole new way of eating or looking. Many meat-and-potatoes high-school kids return from college counting fat grams and eating no meat. The new restrictions throw the family a bit, especially a mom who is planning to fix all the old favorites to please her returning child.

This is where flexibility helps. We faced low fats and no meat, so I tried a meatless version of the family chili recipe, which tasted fine. We all learned something from having a nutritional police officer on duty temporarily, and we maintained a sense of humor, even when most of the contents of our cupboard were deemed unfit.

The issue of appearance seems to press a more sensitive button between parents and college kids. The boy who comes home with an earring in his ear; the girl who no longer cares about clothes and makeup; the boy who doesn't shave for days—these changes often make parents cringe.

"If you're looking for a job in this town, you'll have to take that earring out of your ear," a father tells his son gruffly on his first return trip to his small hometown.

"If they don't like me because I have a gold ring in my ear, I don't want to work for them," the boy replies.

This conflict defines the generation gap. The boy idealistically stands for a principle: "I am who I am, and an earring doesn't change that." The father, based on experience (and an admitted bias), is realistic about the responses of his generation, which does the hiring. He knows his son jeopardizes his chances with his appearance, and he worries about the boy's decision-making ability when he vows to stick to his principle regardless of the outcome. The father wants to protect the boy from the natural consequences of his decisions. He also wants to protect himself from embarrassment.

Two tips helped me in dealing with these differences over appearances and decision making. First, I remembered that college students may undergo up to four personality changes as they seek a more stable definition of themselves, and that those who drift from looking like carbon copies of their parents are apt to come through the process with a clearer self-definition. And that final definition will probably come close to the images they found modeled at home.

The other tip came from Jesus and concerned my unrealistic

expectations about their maturity. I, too, worried about the priorities on which they based their decisions. I subtly expected them to share my priorities about working hard, keeping a car clean, or being at church on time. I expected them to reach nearly the same conclusions about appropriate hairstyles, wise use of time, or qualities in friends. Yet, they had not accumulated the same experiences that shaped my thinking. Was I expecting them not to make mistakes?

"Be perfect," Jesus commanded in the Sermon on the Mount, but what did He mean? In the Bible, the Greek and Hebrew words translated *perfect* mean three things: (1) Be complete, which means to be *who* God created you to be; (2) be mature, or *where* you are, within your set of circumstances and at your age level of maturity; and (3) be holy, which means surrendered to the *process* of growing and changing.

This spiritual insight became an "Aha!" of my parenting, especially in living with almost-grown kids during their visits home as I aim not to confine them in ways that fulfill only my expectations. I'll always remember a friend's remark that haunted me. "I never felt completely free to be myself until my mother died," she said. I vowed then not to confine my grown children in boxes of expectations they can't break out of when they're around me. I'm still vowing to allow them to be themselves, even when that differs from who I am.

When Derek came home with hair longer than mine one vacation, he said, "I'm wearing my hair like this because it's the only time in my life that I can look this way—and I want to try it." He wanted to be who he was at his age instead of acting my age to please me.

Jesus' call to be perfect by His definition reminded me that our college kids are unique and not yet adults but still in process—not finished yet!

Another new issue may be questions about their faith. "How do you know Christianity is the only right religion?" a 20-year-old might ask. "How can we really believe all that's in the Bible?" Such questions might frighten us, as we fear they're drifting away from God, but those doubts may be their footsteps on the path toward owning their own faith. And it may be time to return to R. C. Sproul's video "Choosing My Religion" (see chapter 4).

A minor but interesting issue with our college students was their new perspective on parenting. While away at school, they became instant experts on how to raise the younger siblings left at home. "I can't believe how you're spoiling her!" I heard more than once. "You never took me out for dinner in the middle of the week. You never bought me two pairs of shoes at once. You never let me get away with that . . ." I tried not to overreact to all the new advice, realizing the message partly meant "I miss getting that attention, and it's hard for me to come home and see what I'm missing."

I made one huge request when our college kids came home. I didn't want to hear the remark I'd heard from other returning students: "After being home for only ten minutes, I was ready to go back to school!" Though the comment honestly reflected the difficulty of trying to fit in with old friends and family patterns, I told them their mom would take that statement much too personally. I also cringed when I heard them misuse the word *home,* as in "I always go *home* after my sociology class," meaning the dormitory. *Home* is where we all live together, where your bedroom is across the hall from your sister's, where your pictures are taped on the refrigerator door and the junk drawer is the third one down on the left. Get the idea?

Serendipities

We ironed most wrinkles out of our unrealistic expectations during those first visits home by communicating, compromising, and being flexible—which freed us to enjoy some wonderful, spontaneous celebrations. First, I made a great discovery about

Christmas vacations with older kids. Years ago, as the mother of three young children, I always felt a responsibility to "make Christmas" for our family through special decorations, food, or meaningful activities. I became the self-appointed Chairwoman in Charge of Cheerfulness.

As the mother of college kids, however, I found that merely being together "makes Christmas." It's a blessing we used to take for granted, but now we appreciate it on a whole new level. We focus less on things and more on relationships, with Jesus and with each other. Being together magnifies the meaning of Christmas, and I'm relieved of a great (and unrealistic) burden.

Another serendipitous blessing of this college era at Christmastime is that the Christmas letters we receive from friends in our age group get lots more interesting. Instead of descriptions of who loves soccer and scores goals and gets *A*'s and *B*'s in fourth grade, we now hear about what those kids choose to do after high school, choices that reflect the adults they are becoming.

We've also discovered the joy of making the most of spontaneous moments. Instead of putting on pajamas at ten o'clock, some nights Lynn and I put on our coats and go to the late movies with the kids.

At noon one Saturday, we all decided we'd had enough of this no-fat-grams stuff, so we piled in the car and went to "Burger Madness" at a local restaurant for big, juicy hamburgers. As we sat together around a table, wolfing down those burgers, I knew I was living a moment I'd appreciate for a long time.

One brilliant blue-sky morning, just before Derek went back to school his first Christmas home, he came into the study, where I sat facing a pile of procrastinated projects.

"Let's go cross-country skiing today, Mom," he suggested enthusiastically.

My New Year's resolution flashed before me: *Be more disciplined, and quit procrastinating.* So I faced a choice: Do I drop everything and seize this moment, or do I stick to my planned agenda? I considered the pros and cons for about a nanosecond, because some-thing (Someone!) nudged me in Derek's direction. I shuffled a few papers, flipped on the telephone answering machine, and said, "Great idea!" (That's unlike me, because when the kids were younger, all too often I chose to stick to my planned agenda.)

Within an hour, we were on a mountain trail a few miles from home, winding through tall pine trees on crunchy snow. About noon, we came upon a picnic table in a clearing where we sat down, pulled peanut butter sandwiches out of our backpacks, and talked.

"How do you know what God wants you to do?" Derek asked. "How can you forgive yourself, even when you know God forgives you? Does God really see us as righteous as Jesus?"

Those tough, searching questions had not surfaced around the dinner table at home, but they seemed to come easily as we sat in the midst of God's awesome creation.

I didn't have many good answers, and I don't think we resolved the issues, but what mattered was that we had the conversation—a talk I would have missed if I'd chosen to stay home and plod through my pile of work. The lesson I carried home from that mountaintop is an increasingly familiar one: *Don't procrastinate* means "Don't put off enjoying the moment that won't come around again." That's especially true during their short visits home.

Saying Good-bye—Again

As each vacation draws to an end, I experience the pangs of sad-ness I always feel when I anticipate saying good-bye to them again. At Christmastime, I tie their leave-taking in to the ritual of letting go of Christmas. As New Year's Day nears, I look with a certain sad-ness at the tree I've enjoyed, because the sight of it reminds me that I have to take it down and pack away the decorations.

I dread the job for days, but finally, I bring out the boxes and start the task. By the time I've vacuumed up the last needles, I begin to experience a refreshing sense of renewal. I find therapy in tackling this task I've dreaded, and I realize again that anticipation is worse than reality.

The same is true of saying good-bye to our college kids.

This is an entry from my journal at the end of Lindsay's first trip home:

> Lindsay is in her bedroom packing, because she goes back to school tomorrow, and I can't bear to even go in there. I don't want to see the suitcases. I feel like our dog, who starts moping around the house when we drag out our suitcases, because he knows we're about to leave and he's not going with us.
>
> For the last couple of days, even looking at Lindsay has triggered the same sadness. I remember how excited I felt three short weeks ago when we went to the airport to pick her up. I remember how I tiptoed into her room and gave her a hug while she slept because I adored seeing her in her own bed. Now, the very sight of her—which I've enjoyed so much—becomes a reminder that she's going. I know the anticipation is worse than the reality, but still, the transition will be tough. I'll say good-bye at the airport, and then later at aerobics, I'll feel sad because she used to go there with me. For a few days, her room will echo with emptiness. And I will grieve the transition once more.

A few days later I wrote: "Lindsay and Derek left yesterday, and last night I had a vivid dream. Three little bunny rabbits hopped into our house. They were dependent on me to protect them from our dog, and I ran around, trying to help them . . . but they kept hopping away."

Transitions take time. Anticipation is worse than reality. And I still like hellos better than good-byes.

14

In and Out

One spring day, while our college kids bounced in and out of our lives, I spotted a red fox in the field outside our bedroom window. I was thrilled with the sight.

This hillside where I've lived most of my life has changed greatly through the years, growing from a tranquil rural setting into a suburban neighborhood—except for this field to the north. Sometimes I grieve the disappearance of *country,* so the appearance of this red fox seemed more than a mere coincidence. I saw it as God's gentle reminder that I can find what I really need right under my nose if only I keep my eyes wide open.

The fox seemed friendly. He dug his den in the hillside below our window, and in the early morning light, if I stood very still, I could watch him closely. I named him Freddie, and in a way, he became mine.

One morning, I heard the usually quiet creature making a

strange yelping sound, and I discovered that our dog had his nose down the hole. The fox stood nearby, pitifully pleading with the dog to move on. Later, I learned why. Freddie was really Fleta; she had a den full of babies, and the once-docile fox had been transformed by her new role as a mother. Suddenly, she'd become protective. Bold. Aggressive.

I watched in wonder as Fleta spent the rest of that day searching out a new den down by the barn and carrying her six babies, one by one by the scruff of the neck, to this safer home. I felt a sadness at their distance, but at least I could still see those roly-poly balls of fur frolicking in the pasture. Every day I watched them, worried about them, and bonded to them.

Then as spring turned into summer, I sometimes heard that pleading, yelping sound in the middle of the night. Once I got up, put on my shoes and a bathrobe, and marched outside, determined to help the baby foxes. Of course, I could not. The night was too dark and the distance too great.

The next day, the fox family was gone. At first I couldn't believe it. Surely, they were sleeping. I even ventured down to their hole by the barn. Empty. Gone. I felt strangely abandoned. The field seemed so lifeless without them. Each morning I scanned the landscape, hoping to see a blur of red streaking across the field somewhere. I did not.

Finally, I called a local fox expert for an explanation, and he stated it simply: "They usually move on in their season."

"Will they ever return?" I asked hopefully.

"Sometimes. Maybe."

So that's what I started to accept. I thanked God for the privilege of having them for a season, hoping sometime—maybe—they'll be back. Even in the midst of hoping, however, I looked down at the weeds now covering their den in the hill below our window, and I knew all those growing foxes wouldn't fit together in that home anymore.

~~~

We're living through a similar season at our house these days. Our kids are in and out. Sometimes. Maybe. I've heard this called the "Boomerang Era." The farther we throw them, the harder they hit the house and shake everything up when they return. The longer they're away and the more independent they become, the less easily they're absorbed back into the family structure. At school they feel like adults, but when they come home, they often feel like children again, and that makes them uncomfortable. Though homecomings are good, the transitions get a little more confusing.

Parenting doesn't come as naturally during this in-and-out season. They don't always do what I think they should. They don't reconnect with old friends I think they should call. They aren't interested in attending the Sunday night Bible study at our church. And I'm less sure of my role than I was when they were young. I spend more time asking myself questions like, *Should I say something? Is that appropriate? What* is *appropriate?*

I remember a conversation with Derek about his summer job. We had agreed that our college students had to make a certain amount of money each year to contribute to their expenses; how and when they made it were up to them. This conversation occurred toward the end of his second summer home, as he sat at the kitchen counter.

"I have two weeks of summer left before I go back to school, and I'm trying to decide how much time to work," he said.

He doesn't want my advice; he wants me to listen, I warned myself. *Yet I know he needs to make more money for school next year.* "What are your priorities?" I asked, proud of myself that at least so far, I hadn't told him what to do.

"I want some time off to spend with my friends, I'm trying to work in an overnight backpacking trip with Corey, and I need to make some more money."

Phew! At least he remembers the need for money, considering he's part of the generation that cares more about relationships and experiences than making money. "Here are a calendar and paper and pencil," I said. "Why don't you write down your priorities, figure out how much money you have to make, and then fill in your calendar? It sounds as though you're doing a good job of thinking it through." *Tools and encouragement I can give him. Decisions I can't—even though I'm still tempted.*

Parenting is tricky during these in-and-out years when we bounce between being adviser, encourager, and listener.

The Sophomore Slump

The second year of college is often characterized by a down time known as the "sophomore slump." It catches everyone by surprise, because we expect kids to return to campus and "have it all together."

"I didn't think I'd feel homesick this year," one of ours phoned to say on a rainy day in late September of the sophomore year.

Here are some possible reasons: They're not getting the special help that launched them during orientation at the beginning of the freshman year. They don't feel the same excitement that accompanied the freshman experience—the new classes and new friends—and three long years stretch endlessly before them. They feel pressured to find a major when they still don't have an inkling of what they want to be when they grow up. Their ambivalence about pulling away from home and making it on their own still leaves them confused and filled with doubts. They may ask themselves whether college is worth it or whether they're at the right place.

One college professor identified it as an issue of control: "Many feel little sense of control over their own destinies. They feel trapped by the choices they made freshman year—choices about friends, fraternities or sororities, roommates, and courses. They have to declare a major, but feel constrained by family and social agendas. They are pulled in different directions, asked to make choices and live with the consequences."[1]

I see the sophomore slump as part of a larger life pattern, which is the predictable letdown after a big buildup. It happens to me after a spiritual high at a meaningful weekend retreat, after a great vacation, or upon completing a major work project. I often experience a slump at the end of September, when the exhilarating newness of fall wears thin, which seems a replica of an annual moment in my childhood. That was in elementary school when the sharp points of my new crayons became rounded, my shiny, new shoes got scuffed, and the dreams of how I would be different in this new year seemed hopelessly tarnished by smudges in some of my relationships.

This same letdown happened to Elijah after the spiritual victory of defeating the prophets of Baal. He sat in the wilderness under a broom tree, discouraged, depressed, and tired. He wanted to die. How did he handle his slump? First he confessed his feelings to God. Then he rested, responded to God's presence (an angel), and received nourishment that strengthened him to go on.

Coping with the sophomore slump, no matter when it hits, is an experience that prepares our college kids for life beyond the campus. During those predictable down times, we can listen and offer the nourishment of encouragement, assuring them they are not suffering alone and the slump will not last.

Parents' Role in Academic Decisions

Choosing classes each semester and choosing a major are two big academic challenges, and they're connected, because subjects within a major constitute at least a third of the courses a student takes. What's our parental role in this? Obviously, we know our kids better than anyone else, so we can help them gather information to make those choices. We also can point them toward helpful resources, especially the college advisers who are equipped to aid students in making decisions based on class performance and interest inventories.

The combination of encouragement and feedback from both home and school helps confused students. The important thing is not to squeeze them into some preconceived mold, expecting them to be business majors, computer specialists, or teachers because we're in those professions. We offered our kids advice such as this: "Explore a variety of subjects early on. Choose a few courses because they're taught by great professors. And choosing a major now doesn't sink you in concrete in a certain career. People change their minds, their majors, and even their careers."

Do we ever get more involved in their academic ups and downs? I know one father who says yes and has a good example to prove it. His daughter applied to several graduate schools and felt devastated when she was turned down by the one closest to home. Considering her grades and class rank, she didn't understand the rejection, and the issue began to chip away her self-confidence about applying to other schools.

"You need more information here, Heidi," her father encouraged. "Why don't you call the school and ask why you were rejected?"

"I could never do that," she replied, cringing at the thought of such a conversation.

"Do you mind if I make a call?"

She hesitated. "I guess not," she finally agreed.

He called the person who had signed her letter, recorded the conversation on his answering machine, and provided his daughter with some valuable information that changed the message of the rejection. It seems that Heidi had entered a much more competitive application process than she first guessed (250 applications for 20 spots), that she had received erroneous information about the length and type of writing sample required, and that she could take other courses within the university and reapply next year.

"Sometimes they still need our help in gathering information that makes a difference," this father states.

"Political Correctness" on Campus

Christian students on secular campuses may need help with the intolerance they may encounter toward their beliefs. Two ideologies that reign supreme there today are "political correctness" and "multiculturalism," which embrace diversity and promote relativism, or the denial of truth and moral absolutes. Society reflects those ideologies. Two-thirds of the American people believe there are no moral absolutes, and half as many people today believe the Bible to be true as did in the 1960s. According to the late Alan Bloom, in his book *The Closing of the American Mind,* most college freshmen believe that truth is a matter of opinion and morality a matter of preference. They make choices based on what "feels" right to them.

On the other hand, Christians believe truth is clearly spelled out in the Bible and has "exclusivity" at its core: To get to heaven, you must believe in Jesus and surrender to Him. That belief, which is not politically correct, offends some people.

A Christian who led a Bible study in a secular campus dorm described her conversation with a resident adviser.

RA: "So you're trying to tell us that you think 18-year-olds have found *truth.*"

Student: "Yes, we believe there is *truth* to what Jesus said."

RA: "That's really sad, that 18-year-olds claim to know *truth.*"

To the student, the conclusion seemed obvious: It was fine to pursue *truth* at that university as long as you didn't find it.[2]

Christians on secular campuses discover they will be criticized for their opinions— *and* their right to disagree—even within a subculture that claims to be stamping out all intolerance. Recognizing this double standard becomes part of the students' challenge of learning to live *in* the world but not be *of* it, to recognize both worldly and kingdom standards and choose the kingdom's.

As parents, we wince as we watch our students on secular campuses facing this challenge with their tender vulnerabilities and desire to fit in amidst the lures of strong peer pressures. I wonder if we're preparing our kids to articulate their faith among well-educated people who are, in many ways, hostile to it. Though we provide a supportive environment that nurtures their personal faith in our homes and churches, we rarely discuss the controversial issues that help them clarify their own answers to the tough questions. When our student felt this pressure in a couple of classes on a secular campus, we tried to pass on tools for coping, such as appropriate Scriptures, magazine articles from respected sources, encouragement to call a trusted spiritual mentor, and the assurance that we prayed daily. It was one of those times I felt a bit unsure of my role, but I wrote this letter, beginning with a disclaimer:

I hope I'm not overstepping any bounds by writing you what is on my heart. I think of you nearing adulthood and making your own decisions and asking tough questions in order to come up with your own answers. As your parents, we're in kind of a hard (but exciting) place, because we can't hold your hand, but we can watch and pray and always let you know how much we love and believe in you, especially when the ground seems a little shaky, as it often does in college.

Those tough classes you're taking seem to be your current "battles" in which you can be refined by the heat, as fire refines the precious gold out of the ore. The Bible offers some help in dealing with such battles. I just read this morning about Daniel in the book of Daniel who survived the lions' den, and I noticed he did three things in facing his tough battle. (1) He had trusted friends whom he counted on to pray with (Dan. 2:16-18). (2) He had his own disciplined prayer life that strengthened him (Dan. 6:10). And (3) he trusted God, believing His promises and acting as though he believed Him (Dan. 6:23). Daniel didn't fight his battle alone.

Remember, you're not alone in this battle. Dad and I love you so much and find it truly exciting to stand by you through the challenges of college. We know with deep faith that God is shaping you to a call that is just right for you.

Love, XOXOX Mom

The challenge our kids face is knowing the truth and living it, but acting in love, as Jesus did. It's not enough to change the laws or campus politics; the goal is still to draw others to the person of Jesus, who is in the business of changing hearts. As one of our kids said, "Those who disagree with me know what I believe, but I wonder if they know I care." Speaking the truth in love, with courage, compassion, and clarity, is the challenge in the world today. As Chuck Colson said, "We must first be holy people before we can bring a holy influence into society."

After College—Then What?

At some point in the junior or senior year, we begin—with our children—to think beyond the college years. What kind of world will they enter? Will they be prepared? Will they be able to cope in the next chapter of real life? In *The Postponed Generation*, a book for parents concerned about their children's lives after college, author Susan Littwin described a startling trend among young people: They don't want to grow up. They're postponing the responsibilities and autonomy of adulthood by taking longer to graduate from college, living at home longer, taking longer to find "the right job," and marrying later.

We've been told that our kids are part of the first generation that will experience a standard of living lower than their parents', yet the more surprising news is that these kids are entering the adult world with a disturbing sense of "entitlement" to the good life and good times. They believe they're entitled to meaningful jobs with status and good salaries, freedom from drudgery and frustration, and the kind of homes in which they grew up. When they graduate from college, they're surprised to find that lifestyle is not waiting for them in the real world. They feel confused, unfocused, and dependent, and they continue the identity search of adolescence well into their twenties.

Chuck Colson offers three reasons for this "Peter Pan

Syndrome": (1) our system of higher education, which keeps young people dependent well into their twenties; (2) the current recession, which means young people can't find jobs and can't afford to start their own households; and (3) the coddling from a generation of parents who lived through harder times and learned to struggle and sacrifice, but who want to protect their children from the same lessons. He notes, "Today's children grew up affluent. They're not used to sacrificing for anyone."[3]

The media continually repeat these insights on the "twentysomething" adult adolescents who fear the American Dream is over for them. They realize their expensive educations may not be enough to keep them out of low-paying, low-skill "McJobs," which means they're likely to live with their parents and unlikely to own a home in the next ten years.

The "twentysomething" kids are called baby busters (born between 1961 and 1981). They're the children of baby boomers (born between 1946 and 1964) and the children of divorce (some 40 percent grew up in broken families). They're the latchkey children of neglect and the victims of declining educational standards.

Some experts predict blessings will grow out of those adversities and that this generation will grow up to strengthen the American family. Even though they are marrying later, they will become dedicated spouses who will spend more time with their children in an effort to protect their families from the stresses and distractions they faced in growing up.

In *The Postponed Generation*, Littwin offered advice to young people and their parents. For young people: Develop your minds, and develop ways to make yourselves useful. That demands an interdisciplinary mix of courses on college campuses—practical majors like computer science and business mixed with liberal arts subjects that teach thinking, research, and communication skills. Take courses that lead to employment. Spend time with the career counselors on campus. Seek volunteer work or internships in the summer, or part-time during school, that might identify a career interest. Get your feet wet in the kind of work you might like as a career. Also, learn about the world and its problems; that will distract you from the ceaseless preoccupation with yourselves. We're living in an era where we think too much about ourselves. Do something for other people.

For parents, she advised that we lighten up and realize our kids are not entering the same world we did. We should accept the fact that adulthood happens a decade later than it did for us. College takes longer—on the average of five-plus years now. She wrote,

> Your young adult children are facing a different set of problems, even if their own mind-set is one of those problems. There is little point in resenting the fact that your children are still dependent and confused at an age when you had real adult responsibilities. That doesn't mean you have to enable your children to go on that way. You can stop taking care of their unpaid bills or finding new jobs for them when they get bored. But you can also stop thinking about what they ought to be doing and criticizing them and giving them unwanted advice. You can't nag them into adulthood.[4]

Holy Moments on Home Base

In the midst of the tough challenges of the in-and-out years come some joyous moments when we catch glimpses of their maturity or previews of the exciting, new, adult-to-adult relationships we're forming. I call these "holy moments."

I talked to Lindsay on the phone one day, fretting about some details of her next semester that were totally out of our control. "Mom," she said calmly, "Proverbs 22:19."

She sent *me* to the Bible in a spiritual role reversal to find this: "So that your trust may be in the LORD . . ." A holy moment.

Toward the end of one vacation, Lynn and I took Derek out to dinner. We wanted to discuss his plans for the next semester and summer, which included some tough realities about finances, responsibilities, and possibilities. Our kids have always been surrounded by other students who have more, do more, and spend more, but we've tried to show them that God gives us the resources or creative solutions to do what He calls us to do. We've always found a way to live out His priorities. Derek sat quietly, realizing his plans and hopes for the future were not limitless. Financial realities formed a limit, and God's plan formed another.

When he got back to school, we got a letter from him: "Thank you for our discussion that night at the restaurant. Thanks for money to go to college and lack of money to do everything I want to do. It's helping me ask God what He wants me to do." A holy moment.

This summer, we planned an overnight backpacking trip. Though I've grown more wary of backpacking and camping, I recognized this as an opportunity to draw our family together when we all seemed to be going in different directions. So, early in June, we circled the date in August and invited our longtime friends Wayne and Joyce and their two college-age sons, because we've spent lots of vacations together through the years.

We got a reservation at a backcountry campsite, and on a warm Saturday afternoon in August, we started trekking up the side of a mountain toward Fern Lake. On our backs we carried our sleeping bags, camping equipment, and plenty of food. Lynn, bent over under the weight, seemed certain he was carrying the refrigerator.

We reached the campsite on the edge of the lake in late afternoon, set up our tents, fixed a great dinner of chicken, pasta salad, and brownies, and then cleaned up. Before going to bed, we all lay on our backs—nine people shoulder to shoulder, in a line by the edge of the lake, gazing straight up at the black velvet sky, sprinkled with the brilliant fairy dust of a zillion stars.

"Wow!" someone suddenly exclaimed. "A shooting star!"

In amazement, we all fell silent as we watched the heavenly light show, one star after another streaking across the night sky. Though no one said anything, we all felt God's closeness in that moment, assuring us—through His awesome creation—that no matter how scattered we feel as our kids grow up and go off in different directions, He will always draw us together and toward Himself.

We felt humbled and unified in the hush of that holy moment.

During this in-and-out stage of our children's college years, we stand on the fringe of their lives as both participants and observers, but thankful that both generations gaze together at the same heavenly Father.

15

The Empty Nest

*T*he mountains of Colorado are crisscrossed with all sorts of hiking trails, but among the most famous is the path to the top of Longs Peak. Each summer, hundreds of hardy hikers make the strenuous eight-mile climb to the 14,256-foot summit.

Living a lifetime in Colorado, I always knew I'd climb Longs Peak. The spectacular, snow-covered mountain beckoned me every morning from my living room window, about 30 miles away across the valley and gentle foothills. Before making the journey, however, I began gathering information and advice from those who had traveled the path before me. Though I knew my destination, I didn't know what to watch out for or what to appreciate.

Oddly, I began getting different descriptions: "The Boulder Field is tedious. . . . The Narrows are scary. . . . There's one place near the top where you must look up, never down. . . . Be prepared. . . . You'll get discouraged. . . . The hike is exhausting. . . . The hike is exhilarating. . . .

Don't do it. . . . You must do it!"

I soon realized I could pick and choose the advice that would shape my attitude about this unknown journey. And the same is true with our family's journey toward the emptying nest. With two in college and one nearing the end of high school, our journey from here is personally unknown. We know our destination, and it beckons us. But from here on, we're operating on anticipation, not firsthand experience.

So I've started gathering information from those who have gone before me. Oddly, I get differing descriptions: "The empty nest is a lonely place. . . . It's like a second honeymoon. . . . Lock the door; they keep coming back. . . . You worry they'll marry the wrong person. . . . You worry they'll never get married. . . . Grandparenting is the grandest part of parenting!"

So far, anticipating the empty nest is kind of like anticipating my fortieth birthday. When I was in my twenties, I dreaded the thought of turning 40. But the closer I got to that date, the less dreadful 40 seemed. In fact, turning 40 seemed natural and good. That's partly a choice of attitude and a decision to accept reality. Now that I'm closer to 50 than 40, turning 50 doesn't sound quite so old or bad, either. I'm sure God lovingly builds these adaptive attitudes into us so that we fit into our changing seasons more easily, even as He transforms a ptarmigan (a bird of the Colorado high country) from speckled brown in the summer to snow white in the winter.

Still, transitions can be difficult.

I think of Katy's description of her journey into the empty nest. "Please pray for me," she asked in a shaky voice at our couples' Bible study one Sunday evening in late September. "I've just turned 50. Both girls are off in college this year. My parents are packing up and selling our family home and moving to a condo. They look frail, bewildered, and elderly to me, and I see myself in them. They are where I'm headed.

"I know in my mind this is a good period of life, but right now I feel sad as I look ahead. I fear there's more behind me than in front of me."

We all encouraged her as she finished. She's healthy. She runs several miles a day. She's just earned her master's degree in counseling at seminary and has a nearly full schedule of clients who need her, as does her husband, who had his arm around her as she spoke. She has much to look forward to, but at that moment, she jumped over all those new beginnings to the fear of growing older and the loneliness of separation from her children. She could see only her losses.

We prayed for her and tried to comfort her, but as we left that evening, I wasn't sure we'd soothed that sad and frightened feeling deep inside her. She was in mourning over her losses, and grieving takes time. We don't pass through life's transitions easily. Though we have faith in God's promises, we have human hearts that feel the pain of this world, which includes the pain of separations— from our children as they leave home and from our parents as they grow older and die. We have difficulty adjusting to God's plan that changes families through the years. Though we know our future is infinitely bright, we sometimes struggle in the present.

I stayed in close touch with Katy, and within a couple of months, she seemed transformed into a walking billboard, dedicated to telling the world about the joys of the empty nest. She had a sparkle in her eye that she explained with a near-blush: "Our marriage has never been better. We're enjoying a new closeness and wonderful freedom. On a Saturday afternoon, we can go off on a bike ride or work in the yard and not worry about anyone's schedule but our own. We can buy and eat exactly what we want. I feel great and can tell you that this is a wonderful chapter of life!"

Katy had endured the transition, and her experience fit the premise I stated earlier in this book. She feared and dreaded the family change in advance; she grieved the transition for a period of time; but by God's grace and her choice of attitude, she eventually adjusted to the change and is now entering this phase of her life with renewed energy and great anticipation.

Empty-Nest Enthusiasm

We need more of Katy's enthusiastic messages about the empty-nest season of life. As I've said, I dislike the term *empty nest*, not only because it sounds so *empty*, but also because the term seems to imply that filling the nest is the nest owner's primary task in life. Those of us nearing or immersed in the empty-nest stage know that God has much more in store for us in the future. For many people, that 15-year season between ages 50 and 65 is the most productive and fulfilling of their lives, but those of us coming up through the ranks don't hear that positive feedback often enough.

That doesn't mean the empty-nest season is without its challenges. Each of life's seasons has its special tasks. One is dealing with the unrealistic expectation that when the children are gone, we won't worry about them anymore. The truth comes closer to a line out of the movie *Parenthood*. In the midst of family problems, an elderly father looks at his son wearily and says, "You never cross the goal line. It goes on forever."

When do we stop worrying? The answer is simple: never.

Though our children are out of sight, they are never out of our minds. Once a parent, always a parent. No matter how many miles separate us, we're forever connected by invisible but powerful bonds, and their concerns are still our concerns.

Surely, the state of affairs in the empty nest *is* affected by how many miles separate family members, however. In looking to those ahead of me in this season, some feel too close to their children who have moved back home and now share the same kitchen and bathroom again. Others feel too far away from their children and grandchildren who live across the country. From my point of view, the just-right ones live in the same or close communities, which means they can more readily be a part of each others' lives. But that doesn't happen so much anymore.

Years ago, kids grew up, got married, and moved down the street, and extended families continued to grow up together. But in our mobile society, when a son or daughter goes off to college in another state, he or she may never live in the same community with parents again.

I'm trying to bargain with God on this issue as I keep offering Him this prayer: "Lord, I willingly accepted Your plan to let them go away to college. It seemed right that they grow up away from home at that stage in their lives. But how about if we bring them back closer to home when it's time to settle down? Oh, don't get me wrong. The experience of working somewhere else for a year or two would be good. But I think they'd do best if they eventually settled in Colorado, don't You? Of course, I pray all this seeking Your will. Amen."

Always, after the "Amen" of that prayer, I feel a slight nudge that I've come to recognize from the still, small Voice. And though I can't make out the whole message, I hear one phrase loud and clear: "Trust Me . . . even when My plan is not your plan."

Other issues of the empty nest season include aging and making mid-life adjustments, dealing with elderly parents and kids who move back home, parenting adult children, and anticipating their marriages. When I look at that list, it seems the empty nest comes at a bad time, in the midst of many losses, such as the loss of children when they leave home, the loss of youth as we face the reality of aging, and the loss of our parents as they grow older and die. Yet losses are a part of every season. So are gains, as those who have gone before me describe.

Aging and Mid-life Issues

Do men and women respond to mid-life differently? Mid-life is a time of reflection when we look back and evaluate how we've lived our lives so far. We've already acknowledged that some men feel a sense of regret when they suddenly realize their children are grown and gone, ending a whole chapter of their lives in which they didn't fully participate. Those fathers are on the upper edge of a new generation of dads who are taking a more active role in parenting.

Historically, we see that parenting trends have gone in cycles. Years ago, in an agricultural society, kids worked long hours on the farm alongside their fathers. Important bonding took place naturally. Then came the Industrial Revolution, which took fathers out of the homes, especially during those early years of family life when the kids were young. Now the cycle is swinging around again, as many young fathers recognize the sacrifice is too great and are determined to participate more in raising and nurturing their children. Still, this reversal leaves many fathers at mid-life with a sense of regret.

It's never too late to start, however. "I'm going to live each day with no regrets," one father vowed. "Starting today."

While fathers may feel a surprising sadness about their children's leaving home, they don't seem as emotional about many other issues of this season, such as aging. In fact, maturity benefits a man. According to media personalities and advertising messages, men get *distinguished* and *rugged* while women get *old* and *wrinkled*.

For years, I've worried about growing older and turning into somebody nobody wants to have around. I've admitted that getting Alzheimer's disease is one of my greatest fears. Lots of younger people tease about this illness. Lots of older people live with its painful reality. In between are those of us in mid-life who read about Alzheimer's and feel horrified when we forget a person's name or fumble for a word. *Is this how it starts?* I wonder with a stabbing fear. Sometimes I seek comfort and affirmation from our kids.

"Lindsay, can I live with you when I get old?" I teasingly asked one summer evening just before she went back to college.

"Of course not," she answered all too quickly, with a grin.

"Hey, Kendall," she called to her sister down the hall. "Can

Mom live with you when she gets old?"

"No way," Kendall said, coming into the room. "I always feel sad when I hear about those families where the grandma lives with them, and they take her to the shopping mall and leave her in the car like a dog and keep going out to check on her. Grandmas shouldn't live like that."

I dropped the subject, but they missed my point completely. I don't really want to live with them. I cringe at the thought of that reverse dependency. I merely needed to know that my growing older wouldn't change how they feel about me.

I'm trying to accept the reality and inevitability of growing older, but this is what bothers me: I *used* to be better in many ways ten years ago. I used to run faster and farther. I used to look better. I used to remember what I had on my calendar for next Wednesday afternoon without looking. I've peaked in some areas. I'm "over the hill," and I grieve the loss of my younger self.

As I grow older, I cling to my favorite birthday verse: "Do not lose heart. Though outwardly we are wasting away, yet inwardly we are being renewed day by day" (2 Cor. 4:16). I'd like some parts of my outward body to waste away a little more, but that's not the point of this verse. It means my physical body is aging, but my soul is not. It's eternal, and it's the part of me growing stronger and better every day.

Many women attribute the emotional swings of mid-life to menopause, when the body seems to be at war with itself, and changes in hormones affect sleep patterns, body temperatures, and even the ability to think clearly.

There are ways of dealing with most of those issues. Doctors prescribe treatments to help women through menopause. As for prescriptions for aging, one person offered this advice: "Fix your eyes on one or two good mentors who are aging well—people who refuse to become critical and crotchety, who are still enthusiastic and curious about life and flexible enough to accept changes in the world that are different from their *good old days*."

Aging Parents

The empty-nest season brings a double whammy of losses at both ends of the scale: loss of children and loss of aging parents. Both bring us face-to-face with our own mortality, but it's the imagined loss of our parents that triggers an instinctive fear of being orphaned or abandoned. We also face the emotional responsibility of the role reversal as our parents age. Ellen Goodman wrote, "In middle age, most of us are flanked by adolescent children and aging parents. We are the fulcrum of this family seesaw, and expected to keep the balance. As one set of burdens is lifted gradually by independence, another is descending, sometimes slowly, sometimes abruptly, pulled by the gravity of old age or illness."[1]

The reality of becoming our parents' parents both surprises and stretches us. Most of my life, my mother suffered from emphysema, and I always knew I'd take care of her when she grew too weak to care for herself. So we built a house next to hers, and for the final years of her life, I bought her groceries, took her to the doctor, and helped her in and out of the bathtub.

I assumed I would love her selflessly during her time of need, but I was wrong. Sometimes I grew weary and felt sorry for myself. I remember one particular morning, a few months before she died, when I was sitting by her bed, feeding her breakfast. I jabbed the grapefruit with the spoon, and some juice squirted me in the eye. Suddenly, the tears rolled down my cheeks.

"I'm so sorry, honey," my mother apologized weakly.

We both knew she wasn't talking about the grapefruit.

While my mother was sick, I felt more revealed as I recognized my inability to love as Jesus wants. I spent more time praying, reading the Bible, and mentally walking to the foot of the cross to confess my pride and self-centeredness. I needed to hear Jesus say "It is finished" so that I could go back and start over in caring for her. I had to shave other activities from my schedule to conserve my energy during that time.

When that kind of challenge coincides with children leaving home, we feel fragile and keenly aware of life's losses. Yet in this fragile state, we are quicker to recognize our total dependence on God, which puts us in a place of surrender where we can receive His comfort.

Moving Back Home

"Home is the place where, when you have to go there, they have to take you in," wrote Robert Frost. Though experts come up with more sophisticated reasons, the fact is, many young adults are moving home. *Renesting* is the term for the home that now houses adult children and their parents under the same roof. And if adjusting to the empty nest seems tough, try the adjustment to renesting, friends tell me.

According to statistics, at least 10 percent of young adults move back home between college graduation and age 34. That's a sharp reversal of the trend in the 1960s, when kids moved out on their own as quickly as possible. The reasons fall into the description of the Peter Pan Syndrome, where young adults postpone their real-life responsibilities indefinitely. What usually brings them home, however, is lack of money. They're looking for a job or a place to live, "trying to find themselves," working through a relational problem, or claiming helplessly they "just can't make it." Some divorced kids move home with their own children. As one mother said with a sigh, "We had two kids. Now we're down to three."

Some renesters give a more blunt reason: They don't want to scrounge around in some grungy apartment when they can come back to the comforts of home with free rent, free laundry service, free TV and VCR, and a full refrigerator.

This attitude is the reason parents who have experienced renesting advise the "Three T's" before the first suitcase even comes through the front door: *Take your time, think it over,* and *talk it over.* Most of us want to say yes to our children's needs, but at this stage they're no longer children. They're adults, and adults have responsibilities. Our aim is to continue to help them toward emotional and financial *independence,* not *dependence.* We need to recognize there will be adjustments when two generations of adults share the same home. Both generations get set in their ways.

"Especially take time to think about saying yes to something that could be a problem," one parent said. "In a moment of weakness, we agreed our daughter could get a dog before she moved back in with us, and that was a fatal error. That dog has been the source of most of our conflicts."

Here are some areas of consideration:

Discuss a specific time frame. Agree that the living situation is temporary. Even if the date is fuzzy, tie down a goal. If he moves home "until he finds a job" or she comes back until she "finds an apartment," that might take two years. "Let's aim for the end of the summer" sets some sort of time frame.

Negotiate finances. If the renester has a source of income, a certain percentage should go toward utilities and food, at the bare minimum. Other considerations might include such household expenses as toiletries and phone bills.

Set privacy boundaries. When adult children move home, they face some differences from the earlier years, when they had the run of the entire house. Define the shared and private areas. "My daughter used to come into my bedroom anytime, but now that's where I pray, and I don't want her barging in," one mother said. When a married couple move home, they need to know their area is private also. Don't expect to eat all meals together. Both generations need some of the privacy they had before.

Agree on expectations about household duties. Be specific from the start, because this can turn into a touchy issue later. "My daughter and I divide the cooking duties, and we each shop for our own days and clean up the kitchen afterward," a mother said. "I asked my son to help paint the house the summer he moved home," a father said.

State the intention. This living arrangement is new to both the adult children and the parents, and a statement of intentions seems to set the tone for a commitment to compromise and work out the wrinkles. "We knew we would come up against some problems, but we agreed to talk them through and listen to her point of view," a mother explained. "We told our daughter that she was no longer a child in our eyes but a grown woman, and we wanted to be friends as adults together."

Despite the best preliminary plans, some issues are bound to surface that require honest, loving communication. An accumulation of repeated irritations can explode unless the problems are discussed. The parents must ask themselves, Is this an issue worth tackling, or do we need to be more flexible? Having friends over occasionally may be an issue that merely demands flexibility, but a constantly loud stereo or overuse of the phone probably warrants a discussion. One mother considers a problem for a couple of days and prays about it before she brings it up. Her daughter's dog presented such a problem.

"The dog is ruining the backyard, and we have to find a solution," she said. When her daughter got defensive, the mother calmly clarified, "This is about your dog, Janice, not about you."

A father got irritated when his son kept borrowing tools and not returning them. He came to his wife in a rage one afternoon. "I'll listen to you vent your frustration," she said, "but you need to go to him with the problem." After that, they made a rule. The offended must go directly to the offender in the household and not expect a middle person to "fix" the problem.

"Our daughter and son-in-law lived with us for six months," one mother said, "which gave us an opportunity to learn about ourselves and how to communicate and listen, be patient, and compromise. It also gave us the opportunity to see them as adults. Heidi and I both love to cook, and I've always been her teacher, so I felt dismayed one day when she used her own recipe for quiche because she liked it better than our family favorite. Then I thought, *Why wouldn't she have her own quiche recipe?*

Parenting Adult Children

All you have to do is read the "Dear Abby" column for about a week to see that many adult children don't get along well with their parents. Psychiatrist Harry Bloomfield, who wrote *Making Peace with Your Parents,* claims that 90 percent of adults have an incomplete relationship with at least one of their parents. My parents died years ago, and as much as I miss them terribly, I know that many of my friends are having a harder time living *with* their parents.

Family relationships form our most foundational, intimate bonds and trigger our most passionate, sometimes irrational, responses. When there are rubs in the parent-adult child relationship, often the cause is the parent's inability to accept the child as an adult. The parent continues to treat the adult child like a child, expecting to have control over the adult offspring, which is inappropriate. I desperately hope we will get along well with our adult children, but I know the greatest challenge is still before us— transforming the parent-child relationship into an adult-to-adult friendship.

What are the secrets to parenting adult children? How do we move into that adult-to-adult friendship—and when does that friendship begin? It develops slowly as the parent lets up on the controls and the child gains independence, especially financial independence, which usually doesn't happen until graduation from college. The goal is a relationship free of the entanglements of power and control.

Richard J. Foster gives an example of the freedom of an intimate friendship. His friend told him, "My business, my only business, is to bring the truth of God as I see it and then to simply love you regardless of what you do or don't do. It's not my business to straighten you out or to get you to do the right thing." That attitude develops the freedom of "intimate friendship without a slavish need to please on either side."[2] That's what I aim toward with our adult children.

Chuck Swindoll suggests declaring their independence with a letter: "Most therapists I know spend too many hours of their day dealing with people's struggles with their parents' messages. It has them all bound up. Let's give our grown kids a lot of room, parents. . . . In fact, I would suggest writing each of them a letter stating their independence, saying, 'Now that you're on your own, I want you to know that my trust is in you. My confidence is in God to guide you. And I respect you. You're an adult.' "[3]

Beyond that, the guidelines center on the golden rule:

- Treat them the way you like to be treated and the way you treat your friends. With respect. With love and loyalty, by being there for them in an encouraging—not controlling—way. Don't pry into their lives.
- Don't criticize or offer advice unless asked. Allow each generation of young adults to learn for themselves; that's how you learned best. Affirm them. Don't try to change them—you can change only yourself. Don't expect them to live by every one of your values.
- Don't manipulate them through guilt. Don't help them financially so they'll visit every Sunday afternoon. Don't remind them of how much you've sacrificed through the years or let them think they're responsible for your happiness.
- Don't put too many expectations on them. You need to "get a life" in the empty-nest season by investing in other relationships, taking classes, or volunteering. With your new freedom, you can enlarge your circle of activities apart from your adult children. Don't let them feel they are your only outlet for fulfillment. Talk to them about expectations of the relationship at this stage. Do they want you to call once a week? Do they want a standing invitation to Sunday dinner? Give them freedom to make their own plans, even on holidays.
- Remember your goal of this season. Deparent and allow them to gain confidence in their independence. Don't send double messages that undermine their progress, such as: "I

want you to succeed, so here's what you should do . . ." Though the first part of the sentence says "I want you to be independent," the second part says, "You're not capable of making good decisions without me."

Reaching a comfortable adult-to-adult friendship is a growing, changing process, and it's never too late to make new progress. It starts with an honest declaration of their independence and demonstrated steps of continued letting go along the way.

Wedding Bells?

Eventually, the questions cross our minds: Will he get married? When will she get married? Whom will they marry? Statistics tell us they'll probably get married later than we did, but statistics also tell us they're less likely to make the right choice.

Lynn and I have always told our children that choosing the right mate is the second-most-important decision of a lifetime. (Choosing Jesus is the first.) Building and maintaining a strong marriage are God's will but not the world's these days. When they were young, they used to ask, "How will I know?" But as adults, they probably won't ask us.

We pray they will remember some of the guidelines we've often discussed:

Choose a person who shares your faith. If your mate loves God first and you second, your mate will share your commitment to your wedding vows, especially "for as long as we both shall live." If the word *divorce* doesn't enter your thoughts, it won't divide your marriage. Also, if your mate loves God first, he or she will love you better. Picture a triangle, with God at the top point and the husband and wife at each of the base points. The closer each mate gets to God, the closer they get to each other.

Don't expect to change your mate. Though you'll grow and change some together, assume that what you see is what you get. If your mate doesn't change a bit, will you still love him (her) forever?

Love is not a feeling. Love is an action verb that takes an act of the will. It's a choice. It means caring more about the other person's happiness than your own. It means *liking* each other as well as *loving* each other. It means doing exactly what 1 Corinthians 13 states: "Love never gives up; Love doesn't want what it doesn't have; Isn't always 'me first'; Doesn't fly off the handle; Doesn't keep score of the sins of others; Puts up with anything; Looks for the best; Never looks back, But keeps going to the end."[4]

Parents of adult or nearly adult children walk a fine line when commenting on potential mates. I have two friends who gave vastly different reactions to their daughters' upcoming weddings.

"My daughter's getting married next month, and I'm so excited," gushed one mother. "We're gaining a wonderful new member of our family!"

"My daughter's getting married next month, and early on in this relationship, we told her we didn't approve," the other mother said with obvious pain. "We're now living with the results of having voiced our opinion. We're making the most of a situation we didn't feel was right."

My heart aches for that mother. Surely we take a risk when we offer opinions to our adult children. In most cases, we back off and allow them to experience the consequences of their choices, yet when it comes to marriage, the consequences of the wrong choices are so devastating. Besides, we believe we know our children even better than their prospective spouses. If I felt strongly that my son or daughter was making a serious mistake, I would probably take the same risk and offer my opinion early in the relationship.

We're not there yet, so our discussions are still generic and not aimed at a specific person. I sent our college kids a copy of the article "Finding the Love of Your Life: How Not to Choose the Wrong Mate."[5] It described these six pitfalls:

1. *Deciding too quickly.* There's a strong correlation between marital satisfaction and length of time spent dating. Couples who date more than two years score highest.

2. Deciding too young. The divorce rate for 21- and 22-year-olds is twice as high as it is for 24- and 25-year-olds. Young people must mature and know themselves before they can select a lifelong partner.

3. Overeagerness. Take time to work through the concerns or differences that surface in premarital counseling.

4. Choosing a mate to please someone else.

5. Not enough experience. Get to know each other through varied experiences such as family visits, conflicts and disagreements, and stressful times.

6. Unrealistic expectations. "Love conquers all," many young people still believe, instead of the realistic awareness that a successful marriage requires hard work.

As I teeter on the brink of the possibility of one of ours meeting the person he or she will marry, I find myself feeling both jittery and excited. I know the intimacy of their relationship will close me out of part of my closeness to my child, as it should. It will mean yet another transition. Recently, as I attended a wedding, I watched and listened in a new way. Mentally, I've always identified with the bride, but suddenly I identified with the mother of the bride, imagining all her feelings. It was jolting.

For a preview of what to expect, Lynn and I have watched the popular movie *Father of the Bride* several times. In the opening scene, the father reflects on his daughter's wedding: "You have an adorable little girl who looks up to you. Her hand fits inside yours, and she puts her head against your chest and says you're her hero. You worry about her going out with the wrong kind of guys, and then you worry about her meeting the right guy. And that's the worst fear, because then you lose her."

God tells our young people to leave their fathers and mothers and cleave to their spouses in marriage. As parents, we must honor their attempts to do so by allowing them to put their mates first. Along with the marriage license usually come keys to a house or an apartment that means our home is no longer their primary home. Along with the wedding bells comes the end of the expectation that they will be home for Christmas.

Admittedly, this part of the journey is a bit frightening to me, but most who have gone before assure me that marriage enlarges the circle of a family, eventually including the possibility of grandchildren, and that's the grandest reward of all. So I trust God that when we get to the wedding bells part, though fearful from my perspective now, He will provide the same adaptive attitude and strength that have sustained me each step of the way so far—not years in advance, but when I reach my point of need.

Equipped with the information I'd gathered from those who had gone before, I started my journey up the trail of Longs Peak before dawn one summer day. I didn't go alone. Not many of life's journeys should be attempted alone. My husband and son and some friends came along. We started in the dark and could only see well enough to take one step at a time. One foot in front of the other.

The journey was longer than I thought. We hit some hard places. We came upon some wonderful plateaus where we rested and enjoyed a clear perspective of where we'd been and where we were going. Near the top, we hit a bad storm. I wanted to turn back. I felt afraid, and I couldn't see the end of the journey. But others urged me on. Finally, the sky cleared, and we reached the summit. And here's the surprise: That mountaintop was even better than I expected.

Epilogue

Summer has come again to our house.

We're a family of four this season. Derek is home, an almost-senior who is working as an intern and gathering measuring cups, dishes, and cooking skills in anticipation of moving into his first apartment this fall. Lindsay stayed at school for a summer session, and Kendall is readjusting to sharing her parents, car, and bathroom again.

This family's journey through transition is not yet over. We're still in process, changing shape as God stretches us toward new purposes. In the midst of the changes, I still like to get up to see the sunrise. On some mornings, I sit on a stool at the kitchen counter, where I can watch God turn night into day through the windows to the east.

Later I can sit on that same stool and watch the sun setting over the Rocky Mountains through windows to the west. I like the sunset time of the day.

I recently saw a time line that compared the average length of life to the hours in a day. For instance, if you're 15, the time is 10:25 A.M. If you're graduating from college, it's nearly noon. At 47 years old, I'm at about 5:30 P.M.

I think 5:30 P.M. is a good place to be. In an earlier season, when I had hungry little children, life was hectic. But 5:30 is more serene. The hardest hours of the day are behind me; the best ones are before me. Quieter hours. Time to dig deeper into relationships around a dinner table. Time to read. Time for more meaningful, less-pressured priorities.

I'm thankful I can see God's reminders of sunrises and sunsets out our windows.

Years ago, I copied a quotation on a scrap of paper. It's been so long that I've forgotten where the words came from, but the statement was something about "a door or window opening and letting the future in."

That's what God does on our earthly journeys. He opens doors and windows along the way so we can catch glimpses of His love, His awesomeness, or His plan for our future. We see a family of foxes playing, a mountaintop beckoning, or a child changing into a woman.

Maybe we hardly notice the meaning at the moment. It happens too quickly, or we're distracted. But as we look back, we remember the window and say, "Aha! That's what You meant, God!"

As I look back over the family journey I've described in this book, these are some messages I got from windows along the way:

*Anticipating change is more difficult than living through it, because God is sovereign, and change is part of His plan for us. He loves us where we are, but He loves us too much to leave us there. And He is sufficient. He meets our needs *when we reach the point of need.*

*We experience great grief over our losses, because grief is the privileged price we pay for loving the way God calls us to love. Love is not cheap. Love demands sacrifice.

*As the family changes shape, we expand our definitions of ourselves. We don't get stuck in our past; we let go of the old to make room for the new. We allow the blessings of our past to become part of the rich root system from which we draw nourishment for the future.

*Change demands surrender, and life is a series of surrenders and relinquishments. Surrender means greeting each day with this personal vow: "The answer is yes, Lord. What is the question?"

●Even as we stretch toward change, some definitions stay solidly the same. Even as our children's independence gives us increased independence, we're still dependent beings. I am still utterly dependent on God, because apart from Him I can do nothing, and I'm utterly dependent on Jesus' death on the cross for my righteousness each day. I am also dependent on my husband, Lynn, and our marital commitment to encourage and sacrifice for and cherish each other as we go through this transition together.

●As we finish this transition and enter a season of life without children living at home, we focus not on what we've lost but on what we have left—and what is still to come: "Forget the former things; do not dwell on the past. See, I am doing a new thing!" (Isa. 43:18-19).

Amen!

Notes

Chapter 1

1. Dale Hanson Bourke, *Everyday Miracles* (Dallas: Word, 1989), p. 2.
2. Corrie ten Boom with John and Elizabeth Sherrill, *The Hiding Place* (Washington Depot, Conn.: Chosen, 1971), p. 33.

Chapter 2

1. A. W. Tozer, *The Pursuit of God,* special ed. (Wheaton, Ill.: Tyndale, n.d.), p. 26.

Chapter 3

1. Judith Viorst, *Necessary Losses* (New York: Simon & Schuster, 1986), pp. 210-11.
2. A. W. Tozer, *The Pursuit of God,* special ed. (Wheaton, Ill.: Tyndale, n.d.), p. 28.
3. Charles Swindoll, *Simple Faith* (Dallas: Word, 1991), p. 244.

Chapter 4

1. Paul and Jeannie McKean with Maggie Bruehl, *Leading a Child to Independence* (San Bernardino, Calif.: Here's Life, 1986), p. 29.
2. The video series "Choosing My Religion" is available from Ligonier Ministries at 800-435-4343.
3. Jerry and Mary White, *When Your Kids Aren't Kids Anymore* (Colorado Springs, Colo.: NavPress, 1989), p. 47.
4. M. Scott Peck, *The Road Less Traveled* (New York: Simon & Schuster, 1978), p. 19.

5. Gail Sheehy, *Pathfinders* (New York: Morrow, 1981), p. 35.

Chapter 5

1. Dave Barry, "Last Laughs," Knight-Ridder Newspapers, Feb. 14, 1993.
2. Paul Tournier, *Secrets* (New York: Pillar, 1976), pp. 22, 29.

Chapter 6

1. *Now—High School . . . Then—What?* Boulder Valley Public Schools, 1992, p. 8.

Chapter 7

1. Judith Viorst, *Necessary Losses* (New York: Simon & Schuster, 1986), p. 153.
2. Gail Sheehy, *Passages* (New York: Dutton, 1974), p. 36.
3. Erma Bombeck, *Motherhood—The Second Oldest Profession* (New York: Dell, 1983), p. 30.
4. Ellen Goodman, *Turning Points* (Garden City, N.Y.: Doubleday, 1979), p. 67.

Chapter 8

1. Richard J. Foster, *Celebration of Discipline,* rev. ed. (San Francisco: Harper & Row, 1988), pp. 190-91.
2. Jerry B. Jenkins, *As You Leave Home* (Colorado Springs, Colo.: Focus on the Family, 1993), p. 7.
3. H. Jackson Brown, Jr., *Life's Little Instruction Book* (Nashville: Rutledge Hill Press, 1991), random entries.
4. Max Lucado, *In the Eye of the Storm* (Dallas: Word, 1991), p. 154.

Chapter 10

1. James C. Dobson, Focus on the Family letter, July 1989.

Chapter 11

1. Gail Sheehy, *Pathfinders* (New York: Morrow, 1981), p. 318.
2. Ellen Goodman, "Mother Sees a Room Frozen in Time," *Daily Camera,* April 17, 1990.
3. Judith Viorst, *Necessary Losses* (New York: Simon & Schuster, 1986), p. 212.

4. Ibid., p. 206.
5. Ellen Goodman, "An Empty Nest, a New Beginning," *Daily Camera*, Sept. 16, 1986.

Chapter 12

1. Judith Viorst, *Necessary Losses* (New York: Simon & Schuster, 1986), p. 154.
2. Gail Sheehy, *Passages* (New York: Dutton, 1974), p. 27.
3. Ibid.
4. Viorst, *Necessary Losses,* p. 227.
5. Aimee Bingler, "Mom-Sick," *Seventeen,* Sept. 1991, p. 35.
6. Billy Graham, "Points to Ponder," *Reader's Digest,* March 1993, p. 178.

Chapter 14

1. Karen Levin Coburn and Madge Lawrence Treeger, *Letting Go* (Bethesda, Md.: Adler & Adler), p. 237.
2. "Campus Christians and the New Thought Police," *Christianity Today,* Feb. 10, 1992, p. 19.
3. Chuck Colson, "The Return of Peter Pan," *Breakpoint* (Prison Fellowship newsletter), July 23, 1992.
4. Susan Littwin, *The Postponed Generation: Why American Youth Are Growing Up Later* (New York: Morrow, 1986), p. 251.

Chapter 15

1. Ellen Goodman, "Parents Become Dependent," *Daily Camera,* May 20, 1985.
2. Richard J. Foster, *The Challenge of the Disciplined Life* (San Francisco: HarperCollins, 1985), p. 207.
3. Charles Swindoll, *The Grace Awakening* (Dallas: Word, 1990), p. 50.
4. Eugene H. Peterson, *The Message, the New Testament in Contemporary English* (Colorado Springs, Colo.: NavPress, 1993), p. 359.
5. Neil Warren, "Finding the Love of Your Life: How Not to Choose the Wrong Mate," *Focus on the Family,* Nov. 1992, pp. 2-3.

FOCUS ON THE FAMILY®

Welcome to the *Family!*

Whether you received this book as a gift, borrowed it from
a friend, or purchased it yourself, we're glad you read it! It's just
one of the many helpful, insightful and encouraging
resources produced by Focus on the Family.

In fact, that's what Focus on the Family is all about—providing inspira-
tion, information and biblically based advice to people in all stages of life.

It began in 1977 with the vision of one man, Dr. James Dobson, a licensed
psychologist and author of 16 best-selling books on marriage, parenting,
and family. Alarmed by the societal, political, and economic pressures
that were threatening the existence of the American family, Dr. Dobson
founded Focus on the Family with one employee—an assistant—
and a once-a-week radio broadcast, aired on only 36 stations.

Now an international organization, Focus on the Family is dedicated
to preserving Judeo-Christian values and strengthening the family
through more than 70 different ministries, including eight separate
daily radio broadcasts; television public service announcements;
11 publications; and a steady series of books and award-winning
films and videos for people of all ages and interests.

Recognizing the needs of, as well as the sacrifices and important
contribution made by, such diverse groups as educators, physicians,
attorneys, crisis pregnancy center staff and single parents,
Focus on the Family offers specific outreaches to uphold and
minister to these individuals, too. And it's all done for one purpose,
and one purpose only: to encourage and strengthen individuals
and families through the life-changing message of Jesus Christ.

• • •

For more information about the ministry, or if we can be of help to your
family, simply write to Focus on the Family, Colorado Springs, CO 80995
or call 1-800-A-FAMILY (1-800-232-6459). Friends in Canada may write
Focus on the Family, P.O. Box 9800, Stn. Terminal, Vancouver, B.C. V6B 4G3
or call 1-800-661-9800. Visit our Web site—www.family.org—
to learn more about the ministry or to find out if there is a
Focus on the Family office in your country.

We'd love to hear from you!